The ally Intelligent Languages for Couples

TRANSFORMING HOW YOU SPEAK, LISTEN AND LOVE

Sam O. Opeche

The Six Emotionally Intelligent Languages for Couples

TRANSFORMING HOW YOU SPEAK, LISTEN AND LOVE

Sam O. Opeche

ELISAM PUBLISHING

First published by EliSam Publishing, UK, February 2026

ISBN pbk 978-1-9194335-0-9
ISBN ebk 978-1-9194335-1-6

Typeset www.ShakspeareEditorial.org

Dedication

For every couple seeking to build a stronger bridge of communication and care. May this book guide you to the words your heart needs to speak.

And with endless love and gratitude to my dear wife, Elizabeth. Twenty-five years of walking this journey with you has taught me the true meaning of commitment, showing me daily that love is not just a feeling, but a language we choose to speak.

Contents

Figures and Tables

Preface

As far back as I can remember, I have always been a wordsmith. I have always been precious and deliberate about words, mindful of their profound effect on oneself and others. Anyone who knows me will attest to this. Perhaps it is because I have personally grappled with moments of miscommunication, or maybe I simply know the defining power of language – something about me just understands the benefit of using words carefully and intentionally.

This core essence has inevitably shaped my closest relationships. I have experienced the sting of unkind words in moments of misunderstanding, and I have witnessed how easily a lack of care in communication can tear apart partnerships. This personal struggle, alongside the burden of seeking a solution to this profound human failing, became a defining quest in my life.

That quest has driven my work, from voluntary experiences as a Youth & Family Mentor and Restorative Justice Facilitator, to my professional practice as a marriage and relationship counsellor. My mission to see intimate relationships blossom and gain resilience has led me directly to what you now hold in your hands: *Six Emotionally Intelligent Languages for Couples*.

A quote from my favourite book informs us that 'Life and death are in the power of the tongue' (Proverbs 18:21). My earnest hope is that the framework in this book brings vibrant new life to your most cherished relationship.

To every couple brave enough to do the hard work of love, your courage is my inspiration. This book is my offering to you, and it's a testament to the fact that your courage to learn and grow is a powerful act of love.

Thank you for the trust you place in this journey, it inspires me more than you know.

Sam O. Opeche

Introduction

You opened this book because you know a simple truth: love is not enough.

You may be deeply committed to your partner yet still find yourselves trapped in the same unproductive arguments, feeling misunderstood or drifting apart in silent exhaustion. Why does love, which feels so natural, require such hard work? The answer is simple: we were never taught the language of emotional safety.

Every relationship begins with words. From the first 'hello' to the first 'I love you,' language is how two lives connect, overlap and weave into a shared story. Yet, over time, words can become careless, defensive or absent and, when that happens, even the strongest love can feel strained.

It is easy to assume, as we tend to do, that communication just means speaking the truth, but effective communication means speaking the truth in a way your partner can actually hear and receive. Many people believe that love should 'speak for itself.' Yet love unspoken often becomes love unfelt. Words are more than tools of communication, they create the climate of a relationship. They can bring warmth and security, or they can generate coldness, tension and distance.

Through nearly two decades of counselling and mentoring couples, I began to see a clear pattern. The strongest, most resilient relationships consistently and intentionally practised six types of language. These couples weren't perfect, but they knew how to affirm one another, to listen with empathy, to speak with clarity, to repair quickly, to stay curious and to create a vision for togetherness. This way of speaking love is what I call the six emotionally intelligent languages; those specific dialects that build resilience, trust and connection. They use:

1. Affirming words to recognise and celebrate the good
2. Empathic words to listen to and feel with each other
3. Clear words to speak with honesty and kindness
4. Repairing words to apologise, forgive and heal
5. Curious words to ask, explore and rediscover
6. Visionary words to create a shared direction – and dreams.

Each language is powerful but together they form a complete system for communication mastery. This is your framework, not just to survive the challenges of couple hood, but to genuinely thrive. These are not abstract theories; they are practical tools you can apply immediately: from navigating a late-night disagreement to strengthening your bond with a quick text during a stressful day.

Think about your last difficult conversation. Was it marked by frustration or by walking away? That frustration isn't a personality clash; it's a language barrier. When couples fail to connect, they can retreat to one of two painful places:

1. Wall of Dialogue: conflict escalates because one or both of you are speaking a dialect the other doesn't understand and you are stuck in endless, circular arguments, never solving the core issue
2. Quiet Drift: conflict is avoided by prioritising peace over honesty and you live parallel lives, managing logistics until you realise you've become roommates, defined by a silent, growing distance.

This book is about giving you a working vocabulary to tear down both the Wall and the Drift. It is a complete, practical framework for translating your good intentions into tangible, relationship-saving actions.

By guiding you through each language in turn, this book will help you to discover three practical frameworks – the Emotional Climate Code, the Relational Compass, the Bridge and Wall of Dialogue – to help you reset the atmosphere of your relationship and find your bearings when life feels overwhelming.

Learning these six languages is not about becoming a perfect communicator who never makes a mistake. That goal is impossible. The true objective is to become a fluent builder of relational safety.

Every word you choose is an intentional action. When you master these languages, you don't just speak, you construct a resilient, hopeful future. A small, consistent shift in your language can fundamentally change the entire emotional climate of your relationship.

This book is therefore organised in three parts, designed to take you from mere survival in communication to full, resilient fluency:

- ♥ Part I (Chapters 1–2) sets the foundation by exploring the critical difference between communication based on desire and communication based on safety. You will identify your 'invisible script', the defensive thinking that sabotages your best intentions, and you will learn the essential mindsets needed before you even speak your first new word
- ♥ Part II (Chapters 3–8) is about the core languages and dedicates a chapter to each of the six emotionally intelligent languages. It presents the specific scripts, phrases and therapeutic mindsets needed to translate your loving intention into tangible, consistent effect. This is where you gain your vocabulary

- ♥ Part III (Chapters 9–15) is your advanced field manual, showing you how to apply these languages under real-world pressure by –
    - o establishing rhythms through essential daily, weekly and monthly practices that keep your emotional connection strong
    - o mastering high-stakes conflict using tools that turn fights into genuine moments of connection and resolution
    - o building intimacy by growing your 'positive bank account', focusing on joy, physical intimacy and shared growth
    - o navigating life's great transitions – from children and career change to health challenges – through learning how to fortify your partnership.

Your relationship is worthy of this dedicated effort. Stop struggling to be understood and start learning the language of lifelong love. Begin right where you are. Speak one new word, one new sentence, one new language and you will build connection, intimacy and hope.

Welcome to a new way of speaking love, one that truly lasts.

Part I.
Foundation

1. Why Words Matter in Love

Power of Language in Relationships

Words are small and deceptively ordinary things, but they carry extraordinary weight. We use them every day, often without thinking. Yet, words carry immense weight within a relationship. They have the power to shape mood, influence behaviour and determine how safe or valued we feel because they are more than sounds or marks on a page. In effect, they are vehicles of meaning, emotion and connection.

Words can comfort or cut, build up or break down, heal or harm. They are the threads from which intimacy is woven.

Think back to a moment when someone's words stayed with you over the years. Perhaps it was a kind encouragement that lifted your spirits in a season of doubt. Or maybe it was a careless comment, spoken in anger, that still lingers in your memory. In both cases, the words did not simply vanish after they were spoken; they shaped how you felt about yourself, your partner and your relationship. Since our partner becomes the primary voice in our lives, those moments can multiply until they are repaired by the use of an emotionally intelligent language.

As a person's voice becomes progressively and consistently affirming, empathic, clear, repairing, curious and visionary, it transforms communication from survival to connection. Over time, these patterns of speech build safety, trust and intimacy – not through grand declarations, but through steady emotional alignment.

But when the voice turns critical, dismissive, defensive or withdrawn, the same power works in reverse. Words become walls instead of bridges. Conversations shrink into silence. Slowly, a distance grows, not because love is gone, but because the language of love has fallen silent.

In love, language matters because it becomes the daily currency of connection. We may show our love in gestures, gifts or acts of service, but the words we use (and the tone in which we speak them) determine how those gestures are interpreted. A simple 'thank you' can transform an ordinary act into a cherished moment. But a sigh of impatience can undo the goodwill behind a kind gesture.

As the old proverb goes, 'The tongue has the power of life and death.' In relationships, this truth is felt most vividly.

> " When our words become affirming, empathic, clear, repairing, curious and visionary, love grows roots. When they turn critical, defensive or silent, love loses its voice

Micro-Moments of Language

Relationships aren't defined by grand declarations of love or dramatic arguments. They are built in the micro-moments, those countless small exchanges we have every single day, such as:

- ♥ the quality of your morning greeting
- ♥ the tone of a text message in the middle of a busy workday

- ♥ the first words of apology when a misunderstanding arises
- ♥ the way you choose to say goodnight.

Each is a brushstroke on the canvas of your relationship. Alone, a single stroke is almost imperceptible. Over time, small acts of language build up a picture, either of profound warmth and security, or of chronic tension and distance.

As Dr. John Gottman, a leading researcher on marriage, has proven, thriving couples maintain a healthy ratio of positive to negative interactions, ideally five positives for every one negative. I am convinced that emotionally intelligent words are the most accessible and frequent way we have to consistently tip that balance in our favour.

Why Emotionally Intelligent?

I've come to realise that it's entirely possible to talk often and still fail to connect. Frequent communication does not equal connection. Many couples speak daily but remain emotionally distant because their words lack awareness. Without emotional intelligence, language loses empathy and becomes reactive, a tool for defence rather than understanding. Words alone do not guarantee understanding. Without emotional intelligence, they become noise that fills the space but empties the heart, or worse, sharp instruments that wound instead of heal.

Emotionally intelligent language listens even as it speaks. It pays attention not only to *what* is said, but also to *how* it is received. It measures tone carefully, recognising that meaning lies not only in the message but in its impact.

To speak with emotional intelligence is to ask, 'How will my words land in the heart of the one I love?', which requires:

- ♥ self-awareness – am I speaking from love, frustration or fear?
- ♥ empathy – how will these words feel to the one I love?
- ♥ intention – what outcome do I hope for in this conversation?

Without emotional intelligence, we may think we are communicating clearly yet leave our partner feeling unheard or misunderstood. With it, even difficult conversations can become pathways to deeper intimacy.

Using an emotionally intelligent language is about more than choosing the right words, it is about choosing words that honour the emotional truth of a moment. Language becomes the bridge between the two inner worlds in a relationship. When that bridge is built with empathy, clarity and care, connection deepens. When it's built with blame, defensiveness or silence, even love can feel unreachable.

It's striking to note how we often assume that love alone is enough to sustain a relationship. But love without the use of emotionally intelligent languages can leave partners feeling misunderstood, dismissed or unsafe. It's not just ***what*** we say, it's also ***how*** we say it, ***when*** we say it and ***why*** we say it. Emotionally intelligent languages help us speak in ways that soothe rather than sting, invite rather than isolate and repair rather than rupture.

In moments of tension, emotionally intelligent languages offer a pause, a chance to choose connection over reaction. They allow us: to name our feelings without weaponising them; to set boundaries without shutting down intimacy; and to apologise in ways that actually heal. It's the difference between saying 'You always do this' and 'I feel hurt when this happens.' The first escalates. The second opens a door.

Emotionally intelligent languages are also a form of

emotional generosity. They say, 'I care enough to speak with intention.' They create space for vulnerability, for nuance and for growth. And in a world that often lacks emotional depth, choosing words that reflect emotional intelligence is a radical act of love.

Bridging Language and Words

Language is the broad system we use to give meaning, while words fill in the structure (see Figure 1.1).

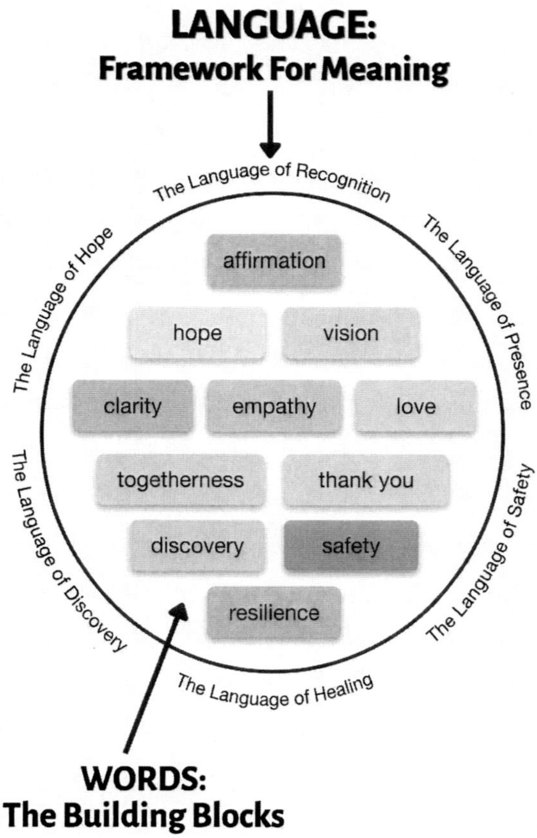

Figure 1.1 Bridging language and words

In relationships, the *language* we choose (affirmation, empathy, clarity, repair, curiosity, vision) sets the tone, but the *words* we select make that language real and felt. A partner may claim to 'speak the language of empathy', but unless it is expressed in attentive words – 'I hear you', 'That must have been hard', 'Tell me more' – the intention remains abstract. To thrive, couples must learn to bridge the two by embracing the larger language of love, and then carefully choosing words that embody it in the moment.

Emotional Climate Code

Every couple lives within an emotional climate; the atmosphere that surrounds the relationship, invisible yet deeply felt. It is subtle and tone, timing and intention can shift it daily. Just like the weather, this climate can be calm or stormy, warm or distant, clear or confusing; it can influence how we dress, travel and plan our days. The words we use create a relational weather system that shapes how safe, loved or understood we feel in that relationship.

Some climates are warm and nourishing, filled with gentle sunshine that encourages growth. Others can be stormy, unpredictable, or even cold and distant. The Emotional Climate Code is your tool for decoding these shifts. It helps couples tune into the emotional patterns that shape their connection, so they can respond with empathy instead of reacting out of habit.

We all know what it feels like to walk into a room where the atmosphere is tense, no words need to be spoken for us to feel the chill. We also know the relief of stepping into an environment that feels warm, light and safe.

When we ignore the emotional weather in our relationships, we risk stepping into storms unprepared. A sharp comment might feel like thunder. Silence might settle like fog. But when we learn to read the climate – when we notice the tension in the air, the warmth in a gesture, the chill in a pause – we begin to understand what our relationship needs in that moment. Emotional intelligence becomes our umbrella, our compass, our forecast.

Here's the good news. Unlike the weather outside, which is beyond our control, the emotional climate of a relationship can be influenced, and even reset, by the words we choose. Needless to say, every exchange, every sentence, every tone contributes to the forecast.

Reading the Weather in Your Relationship

To read their Emotional Climate Code couples are invited to ask:

- ♥ What's the emotional temperature between us today?
- ♥ Are we in a season of closeness or withdrawal?
- ♥ What signals are we sending – intentionally or not?

This is necessary because by learning to read your relationship's weather, you gain the power to shift it. You can bring warmth where there's cold, clarity where there's confusion and safety where there's emotional unpredictability. It's not about controlling the climate, it's about responding to it with emotional wisdom.

If you had to describe your relationship's current climate in weather terms, would you use words that are:

- ♥ sunny – encouraging, affectionate, light, joyful
- ♥ cloudy – uncertain, vague, tense
- ♥ stormy – conflictive, critical, defensive, withdrawn
- ♥ foggy – unclear, avoiding, undeclared
- ♥ fresh and breezy – curious, laughing, new, open
- ♥ gentle rain – empathic, soothing, replenishing.

Couples often find that their 'forecast' shifts daily and sometimes hourly. What matters is not whether storms come (they always will), but whether we have the language to reset the climate when it turns negative and unpleasant.

Words That Build or Break

A careless phrase like 'You never listen', can plant seeds of resentment. A thoughtful phrase like 'I really appreciate how you tried to understand me', can plant seeds of trust.

Words build climate – and climate shapes connection. Couples who become intentional with their language can find that the overall feel of their relationship changes for the better, sometimes in a surprisingly short time.

> " Intimacy is built one conversation at a time. Every affirming word draws us closer; every careless one widens the distance

The Six Language Climate Codes

Each emotionally intelligent language plays a role in shaping the weather of your relationship:

- ♥ affirming words are the sunshine that warms and nurtures making us feel seen and valued
- ♥ empathic words act like gentle rain, refreshing the soul and replenishing intimacy
- ♥ clear words cut through the fog, bringing transparency and safety
- ♥ repairing words calm the storm, restoring peace after the thunder of conflict

- ♥ curious words stir the air like a fresh breeze, keeping the relationship alive and growing
- ♥ visionary words paint a shared forecast of hope and purpose for tomorrow.

By becoming more intentional in these six areas, couples can predict and shape the emotional climate of their relationship rather than being at its mercy.

Forecast Check Exercise

One simple practice is to take a moment to forecast check. At the end of each day, ask yourself:

1. What was today's emotional climate in our relationship (sunny, cloudy, stormy, calm, foggy, fresh)?
2. Which of my words contributed most to that climate?
3. What words could I choose tomorrow to shift the forecast toward warmth, clarity or calm?

To keep track of this, try keeping a simple log for one week. You'll begin to notice patterns – perhaps Mondays feel stormy because you both start the week stressed or Fridays feel sunny because you reconnect. The real discovery is that your words have more influence over the forecast than you realised.

This simple habit builds awareness of the power of language such that, over time, even small changes in word choice can create dramatic changes in the relationship's climate.

Shaping the Climate

Consider Sarah and Daniel. After long workdays, they often snapped at one another over small things: dishes left undone, misplaced keys, unpaid bills. Each exchange added another layer of storm clouds. Once they began practising a forecast check, they realised their evenings almost always felt 'cloudy' or 'stormy.' By choosing to greet each other with a warm word first, 'I'm glad you're home,' they began to shift the climate toward sunshine.

Or take Aisha and Dele. Dele often stayed silent to avoid conflict, but his lack of words left Aisha in a fog of confusion. When he learned to use clear words like, 'I need a moment to process, but I want to talk later,' the fog lifted and Aisha felt reassured.

These may seem like small adjustments, but they radically changed the relational weather.

> " The language you choose shapes the closeness you feel. Emotionally intelligent words create connection; reactive words create separation

Power of Ownership Language

In emotionally intelligent relationships, ***how*** something is said often matters more than ***what*** is said. A single word or phrase can either close the heart or open it.

When emotions run high, ownership language helps keep the conversation safe. It takes responsibility for one's own perception, rather than accusing or invalidating the other person's reality.

Escalating Language (Defensive or Blaming)

- ♥ 'You didn't tell me.'
- ♥ 'You always do this.'
- ♥ 'That's not what happened.'
- ♥ 'You never listen.'

These phrases sound like verdicts. They imply one person is *right* and the other is *wrong*, which triggers defensiveness and pushes the conversation into debate mode.

De-escalating Language (Ownership and Curiosity)

- 'I don't remember you telling me.'
- 'It feels like this happens often; can we look at why?'
- 'My memory of it is a bit different; can we compare what we each recall?'
- 'I might not have understood what you meant, could you explain again?'

These statements acknowledge your personal perspective without invalidating your partner's perspective. They make space for two truths instead of demanding one.

'I Told You/You Didn't' Scenario

A couple is having an argument about something important that was said some weeks back. One insists that they told the other, but their partner insists that isn't true. One partner kept saying 'Yes, I told you'; the other kept replying 'You didn't tell me.' Let's analyse this scenario to identify how language interplay in the heat of the moment is likely to escalate or de-escalate the conflict by examining which language takes ownership and which deflects ownership – and why?

Escalation Analysis

The statement that is almost guaranteed to escalate conflict is 'You didn't tell me' because it is a statement of judgement and fact, which immediately triggers the other person's defensive 'invisible script' (a concept we'll expand on later).

The statement 'You didn't tell me':

1. Violates empathy by making the partner's internal experience wrong. The partner who insists they spoke the words genuinely believes they did, or at least that they intended to. By stating that their memory is a lie or a complete fabrication, their reality is being invalidated. Therefore, the subtext received is, 'You are wrong, and I am right' or 'You are forgetful/lying.'
2. Forces a defensive stance because the statement is presented as an objective truth. The accused partner is forced to defend their integrity or memory, so the conversation instantly shifts from solving the current problem to arguing about the past and the person's character. This is a no-win argument because neither person can prove or disprove the past event.
3. Blocks repairing words, so escalation happens because the language used is accusatory. The pathway to repairing words (apologising, forgiving, restoring trust) is blocked until one person admits they are a liar or deeply flawed, which is not conducive to healing.

De-Escalation Analysis

'I don't remember you telling me' is a statement of vulnerability and personal experience that invites collaboration and problem-solving by:

1. Upholding empathy through acknowledging the possibility that the partner did, in fact, speak the words, but that the receiver simply failed to register the message. It honours the partner's memory while taking responsibility for one's own. Therefore, the subtext received is: 'I believe you think you told me,

but I have no record of it. Let's figure out where the breakdown was.'

2. Activating curious words that, instead of shutting down the conversation, prompt both parties to shift the focus from *who* is to blame to *how* to improve the system. For instance, 'I wonder why that message didn't land with me? Was it a bad time?'
3. Allowing for clear words so that the couple can now discuss the communication failure without the threat of character assassination. They can talk about how the information needs to be delivered to stick, rather than whether it was delivered at all.

Ownership language works because it communicates humility and curiosity. It shows your goal is not to *win* the argument, but to *understand* the moment. It turns conversation from confrontation into collaboration, the essence of emotionally intelligent dialogue.

Practice

> " The difference between escalation and understanding is often a single word, the word that takes ownership rather than assigning blame

From Defence to Ownership

In moments of tension, the difference between *reactivity* and *understanding* often lies in a single phrase. Use Table 1.1 to practise translating defensive, blame-focused statements into emotionally intelligent statements that take ownership and invite connection.

Table 1.1 Emotionally intelligent rewrites

Defensive or Blaming Statement	Emotionally Intelligent Rewrite
'You didn't tell me'	'I don't remember you telling me, can we go over it again?'
'You never listen to me'	'I feel unheard sometimes, can we find a better way to communicate?'
'You're overreacting'	'This feels intense, help me understand what's coming up for you'
'You always make me feel stupid'	'I feel small or dismissed when that happens, could we talk about it differently?'
'That's not true'	'I remember it differently; can we compare what each of us recalls?'

Thought Context

The way a person ***thinks*** – their mental models, beliefs and inner narratives – profoundly shapes the ***language*** they use in relationships. In fact, emotionally intelligent communication begins not with the mouth, but with the mind. Every word spoken in a relationship begins as a thought. Before a sentence is formed on our lips, it takes shape in the quiet workshop of the mind – in our interpretations, assumptions and beliefs. This is where communication truly begins, and where most misunderstandings are born.

Many couples focus on ***what*** they say, but emotionally intelligent communication requires attention to *how they think* before they speak. Words are simply the fruit of thought: if the roots are healthy, the words will nourish; if the roots are distorted by fear, pride or insecurity, even well-intentioned words can sound defensive or distant. Language is the voice of thought. The words we choose are shaped by the way we interpret experience, process emotion and assign meaning to what happens between us and our partner.

1. Perception Creates Expression

What we perceive determines what we express. Two people can experience the same moment and walk away with entirely different emotional narratives. For example:

- A partner who ***thinks*** 'I'm being criticised' may respond defensively
- A partner who ***thinks*** 'My partner is asking for reassurance' may respond compassionately.

The difference isn't just emotional, it's *cognitive*. The difference lies not in the event, but in the interpretation. Our internal narratives filter how we hear and what we say.

Emotionally intelligent couples learn to pause before reacting and to ask, 'What story am I telling myself about what just happened?' This pause allows thought to mature before it becomes speech.

2. Cognitive Filter Blocks Connection

When we enter a relationship, we don't just bring our bodies and our history, we also bring an 'invisible script' – a collection of deeply ingrained thought patterns, assumptions and cognitive filters that dictate our perception of reality. These scripts are often remnants of past hurts or insecurities, and they determine whether we interpret our partner's actions as an act of *love* or as a perceived *threat*.

The crucial thing is that when an invisible script is activated, emotionally intelligent languages shut down. For instance, if your partner is late home, your thought process acts as an immediate filter:

- Positive script (secure): 'They must have been held up. I'll check in'

  - o Result: empathic and clear words are possible
- ♥ Negative script (threatened): 'They don't respect my time; I'm always the last priority'
  - o Result: defensive, accusatory language, which blocks repairing words.)

While the six languages are tools, negative thinking is the rust that stops them from working.

> Language is the voice of thought

3. Beliefs Become Linguistic Habits

Every relationship runs on the unspoken beliefs we hold about love, conflict and worth:

- ♥ A person who believes 'vulnerability is weakness' will be guarded when they speak
- ♥ Someone who believes 'love should be easy' may express impatience or dismissiveness
- ♥ But a person who believes 'love is a dialogue, not a competition' will instinctively speak with curiosity and collaboration.

Our words reveal our worldview. Emotionally intelligent language starts when we question the beliefs underneath our tone.

As Anais Nin took from the Talmud: 'We do not see things as they are, we see them as we are.' Transform the belief and the language will follow.

4. Emotion Regulation Begins in Thought

Emotionally intelligent people aren't those who never feel anger or fear, they're those who notice the feeling before it turns into reaction. Psychologists call this cognitive reappraisal, the ability to reinterpret a situation in real time to reduce emotional intensity. For example:

- ♥ Initial thought: 'She's ignoring me again.'
    - o Reappraised thought: 'Maybe she's overwhelmed; I'll ask gently.'

That one shift in thinking changes everything about the tone, timing and outcome of the conversation and resets the emotional atmosphere.

Thought is the steering wheel; words are the motion.

5. Inner Dialogue Predicts Outer Dialogue

The tone we use with others often mirrors the tone of our internal voice. If our self-talk is harsh, our external speech tends to carry that same sharpness. If our inner dialogue is gentle and curious, our words will naturally express empathy.

Before we can speak kindly, we must think kindly. Before we can listen deeply to another, we must learn to listen to ourselves without judgement.

This is why emotional literacy (personal reflection, journaling, and prayer or meditation) begins with mental hygiene – learning to think in ways that align with kindness and curiosity.

> " Love flourishes in understanding
> – and withers in criticism

6. Thought Sets the Climate

Every relationship has an emotional climate – the overall feeling created by the words, tone and energy between two people. But that climate begins in thought. An anxious mind often creates tense conversations. A hopeful mind invites calm and connection. When your inner thoughts are stormy, your words may thunder. When your inner world is peaceful, your words carry sunlight.

Emotionally intelligent couples learn to tend to their mental climate first – to think thoughts that align with grace, curiosity and truth. Because, in the end, we speak from the atmosphere we live in.

Practical Exercises

Forecast Journal

For one week, keep a simple journal and each day:

- Write down the emotional 'climate' of your relationship
- Note one phrase you said that shaped it
- Write one phrase you'll try tomorrow to shift the climate positively.

At the end of the week, reflect together: What patterns do you notice? How do words connect with your relationship climate?

Three Common Cognitive Filters That Distort Language

Understanding these filters is the first step in transforming how you speak. When we recognise the distortion, we can deliberately choose the intelligent language to override it.

Table 1.2 Understanding filters

Cognitive Filter	Description	Relationship Outcome	Language Blocked
Mind-reading and assumptions	The belief that your partner should instinctively know what you want or need without you having to ask, leading to resentment when they fail	You withhold clear words, expecting them to intuit your unmet need; when the need isn't met, you retaliate with passive-aggressive or accusatory speech	Clear words
Global labelling	The tendency to use extreme, absolute terms (always, never) to define a temporary situation; this catastrophises a momentary failure into a fixed character flaw	This destroys repairing words. Instead of addressing the isolated action (e.g. 'you forgot the milk'), you attack the person ('you ***always*** let me down'), making an apology impossible	Repairing words
Personalisation and blame	The immediate assumption that any negative event or mood is a direct reflection of your own fault or worthlessness, or conversely, that the responsibility for all happiness rests with your partner	This prevents empathic words because all dialogue becomes a defensive exercise. You cannot genuinely listen to their struggle because you are too busy defending yourself or feeling guilty	Empathic words

The practice of the six emotionally intelligent languages is, therefore, the active process of rewriting your invisible script. Every time you consciously choose clear words instead of mind-reading, or repairing words instead of global labelling, you are demonstrating to your nervous system that the threat is not real. You are building resilience by proving that intentional speaking and listening will always lead to safety, eventually dissolving the old, defensive patterns and replacing them with intentional love.

Thought-to-Word Reflection

The goal of this exercise is to slow the process between thinking and talking, so that your words come from awareness rather than reaction. When you feel tense, misunderstood or defensive, pause and complete the table below – mentally or in your journal.

Table 1.3 Thought-to-word reflection table

Situation/ Trigger	**Initial Thought**	**Resulting Emotion**	**Resulting Tone**	**Reframed Thought**	**Emotionally Intelligent Response**
My partner forgot something important	'They don't care about me'	Hurt, anger	Sharp, distant	'They've been under pressure lately; this wasn't intentional'	'I felt a bit hurt when that slipped by, can we talk about how to handle reminders better?'
My partner disagreed with my idea	'They never listen to me'	Frustration	Defensive, argumentative	'We see things differently, but that's okay, we're both trying to help'	'I value your perspective, can I explain mine too?'
My partner seemed quiet at dinner	'Something's wrong with us'	Anxiety	Withdrawn, cold	'Maybe they're tired or lost in thought'	'You seem quiet tonight, is everything okay, or would you rather just unwind?'

Between every thought and every word, there is a moment of choice. That's where emotional intelligence begins.

> The mind is the factory of language. What we manufacture in thought will slip out through the words we speak

Reflection Questions

- When was the last time the 'weather' of my relationship felt stormy? What words made it worse, and what words eventually calmed it?
- What patterns do I notice in my initial thoughts?
- How often do those thoughts assume the worst rather than the best?
- What new thought could help me speak with more empathy, clarity or patience next time?
- If my partner had to describe my emotional climate this week, what would they say?
- Which of the six languages feels like my natural strength, and which one could help reset my climate more often?
- What do I tend to think *before* I speak in moments of tension?
- What belief or story might be shaping my words right now?
- How would it change my relationship if I began forecasting daily?
- What story do I tell myself when my partner disappoints or misunderstands me?
- How could I reframe that thought before I respond next time?

Closing Thought

The Emotional Climate Code is not about chasing endless sunshine, it reminds us that words are not neutral. Every couple faces storms but, by using emotionally intelligent languages, we can reset the climate toward safety, warmth and intimacy. It is not just about controlling the forecast of your relationship, it is also about becoming fluent in the languages that bring balance, repair and renewal. Just as skilled navigators read the weather and adjust their sails, couples can learn to read their climate and choose words that reset the atmosphere.

In essence, your words are your forecast tools. They can predict rain or bring out the sun.

2. Birth of The Six Emotionally Intelligent Languages

Where the Idea Began

Every powerful framework begins with a question. For me, it was: Why do couples who love each other deeply still struggle to communicate in a way that nurtures their bond?

I had seen couples who clearly cared for one another but whose words left them hurt, confused and distant. I had also seen couples who, even in the midst of difficulties, managed to speak to one another in a way that brought healing, hope and resilience. I found that the difference was not their level of love or commitment, it was their language.

This made me realise that couples needed not just languages of *expression*, but languages for *resilience*. Many understood how to express affection, but fewer knew how to navigate conflict, repair wounds or build a long-term vision together. That was the gap.

This realisation led me on a journey of observation, study and practice. Through my work as a counsellor and mentor, and through countless conversations with couples, I began to notice recurring patterns. Certain ways of speaking consistently brought life, while others drained it. Out of these patterns emerged what I now call the six emotionally intelligent languages. They weave emotional awareness, practical communication skills and relational wisdom into a powerful framework. Together, these six languages form a toolkit that helps couples shift from reactive patterns to emotionally responsible connections. They empower us to respond to the emotional climate we're in and to change the forecast gently toward warmth, safety and deeper understanding.

Moving Beyond Love Languages

When Gary Chapman introduced *The 5 Love Languages*, he fundamentally transformed how couples around the world understood and expressed affection. His insight was both profound and essential: not everyone receives love in the same way. For millions, his framework was a genuine breakthrough, helping partners finally see and meet each other's core needs for connection.

However, as valuable as the love languages are, they primarily address how love is expressed and received in times of peace. They don't fully equip couples for the inevitable difficulties in a long-term relationship. They don't provide a complete manual for what happens when trust is broken, when conflict damages communication, when misunderstandings leave you feeling utterly alone, or when you need to collaboratively build a shared vision for the future.

This is where *The Six Emotionally Intelligent Languages for Couples* comes in. Its framework does not replace the love languages; it expands the conversation into the realms of resilience and repair. It provides you with a comprehensive communication toolkit for every season of your relationship. These languages offer a vocabulary for the messiness of real life, not just for expressing affection, but also for:

- ♥ repairing conflict with humility and grace

- clarifying needs without resorting to blame (using clear words)
- sustaining curiosity about a partner who is always changing (using curious words)
- creating a shared future through purposeful discussion (using visionary words).

Emotionally intelligent languages describe how we speak love in the face of everyday challenges, expanding the scope for growth, resilience and deep renewal in your relationship. This system is designed to give you the precise words you need to build a bridge with dialogue and to ensure that your partnership doesn't flounder on the rocks of poor communication.

Why Six?

The number is not arbitrary. Again and again, I observed that those couples who thrived consistently drew from six distinct language modes, using words that are:

- **Affirming** – noticing, encouraging, appreciating; to ensure partners feel valued
- **Empathic** – listening, validating, feeling; to ensure partners feel heard
- **Clear** – expressing needs directly and respectfully; to ensure partners feel understood
- **Repairing** – apologising, forgiving, restoring trust; to ensure partners can heal after conflict
- **Curious** – asking, exploring, staying open; to ensure partners keep rediscovering each other

- ♥ **Visionary** – dreaming, planning and setting direction together; to ensure partners move forward with a shared purpose.

These six form a balanced system. Each one fills a vital role. Remove one and the relationship becomes unbalanced. Together, they create a connection that can withstand stress and change. They are the building blocks of relational intelligence. For example:

- ♥ Too much affirmation without empathy can feel shallow
- ♥ Clarity without curiosity can come across as harsh
- ♥ Repair without vision can fix problems but leave no forward direction.

> " The emotionally intelligent languages describe how we speak love in the face of everyday challenges

When these six languages are present in harmony, a relationship gains:

1. Resilience, the power to withstand – resilience is the ability of your relationship not just to survive conflict, but also to grow stronger because of it. This resilience is born from the combination of empathic words, which validate pain and reduce defensiveness, and repairing words, which restore trust and rebuild safety after a rupture. This partnership ensures that when misunderstandings inevitably occur they don't fracture the foundation. Instead, they become temporary setbacks that the couple is equipped to overcome, turning challenges into opportunities for greater understanding.

2. Depth, the foundation of intimacy – depth refers to the profound level of intimacy and security shared between partners, the feeling of truly being known. This is built daily through affirming words, which consistently express appreciation and value, and curious words, which ensure neither partner stops exploring the ever-changing inner world of the other. The deliberate use of clear words then provides the safety needed for both partners to express their most vulnerable needs, cementing an authentic connection that goes far beyond surface-level interactions.
3. Momentum, the trajectory of a shared future – momentum is the feeling that the relationship is actively moving forward, rather than stalling under the weight of the present. This trajectory is entirely powered by visionary words, the language used to co-create ambitious, exciting and realistic plans for the future. The couple becomes free to focus their energy outward, defining a shared direction and building a life that both partners are equally excited to pursue.

Discovery in Real Life

Let me share a story.

James and Linda had been married for seven years. They loved one another deeply, but their conversations often ended in frustration. Linda wanted James to notice her efforts around the house, but he rarely affirmed her. James wanted Linda to listen when he shared his work challenges, but she often moved quickly to problem-solving instead of empathy.

When I introduced them to the six languages, it was as if a light turned on. James began practising affirmation, 'I noticed you stayed up late to prepare that meal for us. Thank you.' Linda began offering empathy, 'That must have been hard to face at work today. I hear how stressed you feel.'

These small shifts began to change their climate. Later, they added clear words ('I need some help tonight'), repairing words ('I'm sorry for snapping at you'), curious words ('What's one thing you wish we could do differently this month?') and visionary words ('Where would you love us to be in five years?'). Over time, their entire communication dynamic transformed.

> Together, these six emotionally intelligent languages form a balanced system

Framework for Every Couple

The beauty of the six languages is that they are universal and adaptable tools for connection, whether you are newly dating, preparing for marriage, recently married or decades into your relationship:

- ♥ Dating couples can use them to build healthy patterns early on
- ♥ Married couples can use them to repair and refresh long-term bonds
- ♥ Couples in conflict can use them as bridges back to one another.

The framework is not about adding pressure to 'speak perfectly' but about offering a map. If one area feels weak, you know where to strengthen. If one dimension is missing, you know what to practice. For example:

- ♥ In moments of joy, you might use affirming words
- ♥ In moments of pain, you might need empathic words
- ♥ When things are unclear, you'll need clear words
- ♥ After conflict, repairing words become essential

- To avoid stagnation, you'll lean on curious words
- To build momentum, you'll need visionary words.

Every relationship will need one of the six emotionally intelligent languages at different times. Some moments call for empathy, others for clarity. Sometimes we need repair after rupture, at other times we need vision to guide us. The more fluent we become in these languages, the more emotionally agile we become – able to respond with intention rather than react from habit.

Fluency isn't about perfection. It's about presence. It's about knowing which language to reach for when the emotional climate shifts. When couples learn to speak affirming words, empathic words, clear words, repairing words, curious words and visionary words with ease, they build a relationship that's not just resilient, but is also deeply fulfilling. One where emotional safety is felt, growth is shared and love is spoken fluently.

Emotional Climate Connection

Remember the Emotional Climate Code in Chapter 1? The six languages are the emotional regulators that help couples adjust the atmosphere between them with intention and care. Whether the relationship feels chilly from distance, foggy through confusion or overheated with tension, these languages offer ways to warm, refresh, clear, calm, stir and direct the emotional climate.

Each language plays a unique role:

- Affirmation words brighten and warm the space with appreciation and emotional safety
- Empathic words calm the air, soothing emotional storms with understanding

- Clear words remove the fog, bringing transparency and trust
- Repairing words refresh the atmosphere after rupture, restoring connection
- Curious words stir movement, inviting exploration and emotional depth
- Visionary words inspire, guiding the relationship toward shared growth.

When couples learn to use these languages fluently, they gain the ability to respond to emotional shifts with wisdom, not just to react to them. They become co-creators of their relational climate, able to nurture warmth, restore calm and build a future that feels emotionally safe and deeply connected.

Together, they reset the weather of your relationship.

> " Clear words provide the safety needed for both partners to express their most vulnerable needs, cementing an authentic connection that goes far beyond surface-level interaction

Transforming How We Speak, Listen and Love

1. Affirming Words: The Language of Recognition

Affirming words are the conscious and habitual acts of noticing, encouraging and expressing specific appreciation, ensuring that partners feel fundamentally valued, celebrated and seen for who they are.

Central Challenge: Why We Stop Noticing

Affirmation is the oxygen of a relationship, yet most couples allow it to become stale through what is known as negativity bias. Our brains are wired to notice threats and problems, meaning partners often become vocal only when something is wrong (a complaint, an error, an unmet expectation). This creates an emotional debt in which positive contributions are silently taken for granted, and the only time a partner speaks is to criticise. This cycle makes the other person feel as though their worth is conditional, which erodes the safe foundation required for love.

Transformation: Conditional Praise to Unconditional Value

The power of affirming words lies in intentionally flipping this negative script. By actively practising positive focus, you inoculate the relationship against everyday stress. This language is not about flattery. It is about confirming the reality of your partner's goodness, effort and value. Such a commitment transforms how you listen by shifting your focus from faults to qualities.

> " Fluency isnt about perfection.
> Its about presence

Three As of Affirmation

1. Acknowledge (transforming how you listen): actively listen for and notice effort, not just the result. Affirmation starts internally, by seeking out the moments of grace, kindness or hard work that your partner displays throughout the day

- Example: 'I really saw how hard you worked on that presentation today, even though you didn't get the outcome you wanted. Your effort was brilliant.'

2. Appreciate (transforming how you speak): express specific, detailed gratitude for their character, not just their actions. This transforms how you speak by moving beyond 'Thanks for doing the laundry' to articulating the impact of their action on you

    - Example: 'I appreciate how reliable you are. Knowing you always tackle those chores without me asking makes me feel calm and taken care of. It shows me you respect my time.'

3. Advocate (transforming how you love): publicly champion and encourage your partner's identity, dreams and potential, especially in front of others. This is the ultimate signal of love and belief. You become their most ardent supporter and their safety net for ambition

    - Example (to a friend, with the partner present): 'He's absolutely brilliant at his new creative venture; I'm so excited to watch him build that business. I believe in him completely.'

When you consistently use the Three As, you create a relationship saturated with positive regard, actively replacing insecurity with worth and transforming how you speak, listen and love.

> " Affirmation is the oxygen of a relationship

2. Empathic Words: The Language of Presence

Empathic words are the active process of listening, validating and feeling *with* your partner, ensuring that they feel entirely seen, heard and accepted in their emotional truth.

Central Challenge: Why We Struggle to Listen

Most couples mistakenly believe listening means waiting for a pause so they can offer a solution, a story of their own or a minimising reassurance ('It's not that bad'). This 'fix-it' reflex is the biggest blocker to true connection. When a partner is met with advice instead of acceptance, they feel dismissed and isolated. The true challenge is shifting from being a problem-solver to being an emotional witness, a fundamental transformation in how to relate.

Transformation: Fixing to Validating

The power of empathic words lies in confirming your partner's emotional reality, even if you don't agree with the facts of the situation. This signals profound respect and builds the unshakeable safety required for lasting love.

Three Vs of Validation

1. Venting (transforming how you speak/listen): create a secure and non-judgemental space that allows your partner to express their raw, unfiltered emotion without interruption, deflection or cross-examination. This is about making space for them to speak their truth completely
    - Example: Nodding, maintaining eye contact and saying, 'Tell me more about that. I'm just here to listen.'

2. Verification (transforming how you listen): consciously reflect and paraphrase the emotion you heard, showing that the message has landed precisely. This is the moment you actively listen with empathy, not analysis
   - Example: 'So, if I'm hearing you correctly, you feel utterly furious that your manager didn't back you up, and now you feel hung out to dry.'
3. Vindication (transforming how you love): acknowledge the legitimacy of the feeling, confirming that their emotional reaction makes sense. This is the ultimate signal of love – the feeling is valid, no matter what
   - Example: 'Honestly, that sounds completely understandable. Anyone would feel that level of rage in that situation. You have a right to feel this way.'

When you consistently use the Three Vs, listening becomes a powerful act of intimate support, replacing defensiveness with radical presence and actively transforming how you speak, listen and love.

> " The power of empathic words lies in confirming your partners emotional reality

3. Clear Words: Language of Safety

Clear words commit to expressing personal needs, boundaries and emotional states directly, respectfully and without ambiguity, ensuring that partners always feel understood and seen in the relationship.

Central Challenge: Trap of Assumption

The most significant barrier to clear communication is the

deeply ingrained belief that our partner should 'just know' what we need or what we are feeling. This assumption of mind-reading is the silent killer of intimacy. When we assume, we refuse to speak clearly, instead resorting to hints, passive aggression or silence, and then become resentful when the partner fails to meet the unstated demand. This forces the partner to guess, which leads to frustration, misinterpretation and a fundamental breakdown of the trust necessary for sustained love.

Transformation: Ambiguity to Directness

The power of clear words is that they replace the vulnerability of ***assuming*** with the strength of ***requesting***. This language makes the abstract concrete, allowing both partners to negotiate, collaborate and meet needs successfully. By honouring your partner with clarity, you show respect for their time and intelligence, which fundamentally transforms how you listen and respond to them.

Three Cs of Clarity

1. Concision (transforming how you speak): state your need, boundary or feeling using direct, first-person language (I feel, I need). This transforms how you speak by eliminating vague complaints or blame-casting (You always do X)
    - Example: Instead of, 'This kitchen is always a mess', use 'I feel stressed when the dishes pile up. Could we agree to clear the sink before we go to bed?'
2. Context (transforming how you listen): before making a request, acknowledge any relevant context or difficulty your partner might be experiencing. This shows you have listened to their situation and aren't making a demand in a vacuum

   - Example: 'I know you've had a really challenging week at work and are exhausted, but I need us to organise a time for a date next week, otherwise I feel disconnected from you.'

3. Collaboration (transforming how you love): after stating the need, immediately invite your partner into the solution-finding process. This is the ultimate signal of love – you are seeking a joint success, not demanding unilateral compliance
   - Example: 'This is what I need. How does that sound to you, and what part of that request feels most achievable for you right now?'

When you consistently use the Three Cs, your relationship becomes a transparent, safe negotiation, actively replacing fear and resentment with understanding and mutual respect, thereby transforming how you speak, listen and love.

> " The mind-reading assumption is a silent killer of intimacy

4. Repairing Words: Language of Healing

Repairing words commit to apologising, forgiving and actively restoring trust, ensuring that partners can genuinely heal and strengthen their bond after conflict or hurt.

Central Challenge: Vicious Defensive Cycle

When conflict strikes, the human instinct is to self-protect. This leads to the 'blame barrier,' where both partners retreat into defensiveness, arguing over who is 'right' or 'wrong,' instead of addressing the emotional impact. A failed apology often involves minimisation ('I'm sorry you feel that way') or conditionality ('I'm sorry, but you started it'). These types of non-apologies prevent genuine healing, leaving emotional wounds open and signalling to the partner that their pain is less important than your need to avoid accountability. Without true repair, the relationship cannot build the resilience needed for sustained love.

Transformation: Self-Protection to Shared Accountability

The power of repairing words lies in transforming conflict from a destructive power struggle into a relationship-building process. When you take true responsibility for the *impact* of your actions (regardless of your intention), you instantly restore safety and stop the argument's emotional escalation. This commitment transforms how you listen by prioritising your partner's hurt over your own need to be faultless.

Three Rs of Repair

1. Receptivity (transforming how you listen): before you speak, listen actively to the specific impact of your actions or words on your partner's emotional state. Your only job is to receive their pain without defensiveness, self-justification or interruption
    - Example: 'I hear that when I cancelled our plans, you felt completely dismissed and unimportant. Thank you for telling me how much that hurt you.'
2. Responsibility (transforming how you speak): offer an unequivocal, non-conditional apology. This transforms how you speak by naming the specific action, validating their feeling and expressing sincere regret. The focus must be entirely on the hurt you caused

- o Example: 'I am truly sorry that I completely overlooked our anniversary. That was thoughtless and unacceptable, and it made you feel unloved. I take full responsibility for that mistake.'

3. Restoration (transforming how you love): planned collaborative action to rebuild trust. This signals love by demonstrating that the repair is ongoing and future focused. Agree on a concrete plan to prevent the same issue, proving the apology is backed by future behaviour change

   - o Example: 'I want to fix this. To prevent this happening again, I am going to put a recurring reminder on my phone, and I'd like us to organise a special celebration this weekend. What specific steps would help you trust me more?'

When you consistently use the Three R's, conflict becomes an opportunity for deep growth, actively replacing damage with dependable safety and dramatically transforming how you speak, listen and love.

> " Without true repair, the relationship cannot build the resilience needed for sustained love

5. Curious Words: Language of Discovery

Curious words involve the conscious act of asking, exploring and staying open to your partner's internal world, ensuring that you keep rediscovering each other and foster intellectual and emotional intimacy.

Central Challenge: Familiarity Trap

The greatest threat to long-term passion is the familiarity trap. Over time, partners mistakenly believe they already know everything there is to know about each other. We replace genuine inquiry with comfortable assumptions, allowing the relationship to become transactional and predictable. We stop listening intently and stop asking questions that require anything more than a one-word answer. This lack of active curiosity signals a form of emotional disengagement, which breeds boredom and stagnation, slowly eroding the dynamic energy required for sustained love.

Transformation: Assumption to Active Inquiry

The power of curious words is that they are an explicit, daily signal that your partner is still worth your focused attention and that you expect them to be continually growing and changing. Curiosity transforms the relationship into a lifelong expedition rather than a fixed destination. This commitment revitalises how you listen by forcing you to put down your internal narrative and be fully present.

Three Ds of Discovery

1. Deliberate questioning (transforming how you speak): commit to asking questions that require narrative answers, focusing on *why* and *how*, rather than *what*. This transforms how you speak by moving beyond surface-level exchanges (e.g. about logistics or chores) to explore motivations and emotions
    - Example: Instead of, 'Did you get that project done?' use, 'What part of that project felt most challenging, and what did you do that surprised yourself today?'

2. Dedicated presence (transforming how you listen): listen with your entire body and mind. This means putting down devices, making eye contact and listening for the emotional colour of their answer, not just the factual content. Your only goal is to facilitate more discovery
    - Example: 'I hear the frustration in your voice when you talk about your mother. Is there something about that situation that feels really unfair to you?'
3. Dynamic exploration (transforming how you love): apply curiosity to your shared life together by exploring new concepts, interests or activities based on their current passions. This signals love by showing that you are invested in their future growth and that you are willing to evolve alongside them
    - Example: 'You mentioned you were reading a lot about stoicism recently. What is the one core idea from that philosophy you want us to try applying to our weekend plans?'

When you consistently use the Three Ds, they ensure the relationship remains a source of novelty and deep connection, actively replacing stagnation with shared growth, and dynamically transforming how you speak, listen and love.

> Curiosity transforms the relationship into a lifelong expedition rather than a fixed destination

6. Visionary Words: Language of Hope

Visionary words involve actively dreaming, planning and setting direction together, ensuring that both partners feel they are moving forward with a shared, exciting purpose, thereby deepening commitment and fostering collective momentum.

Central Challenge: Drift of Routine

The biggest threat to long-term love and commitment is the drift of routine. When couples stop actively discussing and defining their joint future, the relationship risks becoming a co-managed administrative unit – focused only on bills, chores and immediate logistics. This lack of shared, inspiring goals leads to a feeling of stagnation and a loss of identity as a couple. Without a defined future to build toward, partners can feel isolated in their individual journeys, eroding the excitement and sense of shared destiny required for sustained, passionate love.

Transformation: Stagnation to Shared Destiny

The power of visionary words is that they transform the relationship from a static state into an ongoing, dynamic project. By regularly taking time to articulate and listen to each other's hopes, you restore the feeling of being a unified team working toward a common goal. This commitment makes the relationship feel like an adventure again and provides a powerful motivation to navigate present challenges.

Three Vs of Visualising

1. Vivid articulation (transforming how you speak): express your personal long-term hopes, fears and desired achievements using rich, sensory detail. This transforms how you speak by moving beyond simple statements of intent (e.g. 'I want to retire early') to painting a complete picture of your life's deepest meaning
    - Example: 'My ideal future isn't just about retiring; it's about having the financial freedom to spend three

months a year volunteering together in Cornwall, teaching creative writing to local kids.'

2. Valued alignment (transforming how you listen): actively listen to your partner's articulated vision and look for the overlaps. Your job is not to critique or correct, but to find the common ground where your two futures can merge into one compelling narrative. This is the deepest act of relational listening
   - Example: 'I love the idea of volunteering in Cornwall. I hadn't thought of it, but it aligns perfectly with my goal of having a slower-paced, community-focused life. Let's start a dedicated folder for that plan.'
3. Visible planning (transforming how you love): translate the shared dream into concrete, achievable, short-term actions. This signals love by demonstrating that the dream is real and that you are willing to start making sacrifices or adjustments today to ensure the future vision is secured
   - Example: 'If that's our goal, we need to organise a budget meeting once a month specifically to track our savings for that Cornwall trip. I'll book the next one in the calendar now.'

When you consistently use the Three Vs, you ensure your relationship is always aligned and forward-moving, actively replacing complacency with shared momentum, powerfully transforming how you speak, listen and love.

> " The power of visionary words is that they transform the relationship from a static state into an ongoing, dynamic project

Practical Exercise

Language Self-Check

Take a piece of paper and draw six columns, one for each language. Over the next week, mark each time you use one of them intentionally in your relationship. For example:

- When you affirm your partner, mark 'Affirmation'
- When you listen with empathy, mark 'Empathy'
- When you make a clear request, mark 'Clarity.'

At the end of the week, step back and look at the balance. Sit with your partner and rate yourselves (individually and as a couple) on each of the six languages from 1–10. Then discuss:

- Which language are we strongest in?
- Which language do we struggle with?
- Which language do we most need to practise this season?

This exercise provides a starting point for the journey ahead. Remember, the goal is not perfection, but awareness.

Reflection Questions

- Which of the six languages do I naturally use most often? Which do I struggle with?
- During our last disagreement, which languages were missing that might have helped resolve it faster?
- If my partner had to guess my strongest language, what would they say?

- ♥ Which language would make the biggest difference in our relationship if I strengthened it this month?
- ♥ Which one feels most unfamiliar or uncomfortable?
- ♥ How might our relationship change if we grew fluent in all six languages?

Closing Thought

The birth of the six emotionally intelligent languages was not about creating another relationship theory but about giving couples a living, breathing framework to change their daily interactions.

These languages remind us that connection is not automatic, it is built through intentional, daily words. Words are powerful, but when used with emotional intelligence, they become more than communication – they become connection, repair and vision.

This chapter invited you to see your conversations differently; not as random exchanges, but as opportunities to practise one of the six life-giving languages.

In essence, love grows when we speak its languages with intelligence, kindness and purpose.

In the chapters ahead, we explore each language in depth, and offer practical tools to make them a natural part of your everyday life together.

Read on!

Part II.
Core Languages

3. Affirming Words

Why Affirmation Matters

Affirming words are the language of recognition. At its core, it says: 'I see you; I value you; I am glad you are here.'

In every human being is a fundamental longing to be seen, valued and appreciated. Affirming words answer this longing. They say, 'I notice you, I appreciate you and you matter to me.'

In relationships, affirmation functions like sunshine on a garden. It warms, nourishes and encourages growth. When affirmation is present, partners feel noticed, appreciated and encouraged. When it is absent, couples often drift into criticism, comparison or coldness. Over time, this can erode confidence and intimacy, causing even the strongest of relationships to wither under the chill of neglect or criticism.

It's easy to assume that our partner 'already knows' how we feel. But affirmation is not about stating the obvious; it is about refreshing the connection. Just as we don't eat once and remain full for life, we don't affirm once and expect our partner to live on it forever. Affirmation must be repeated, replenished and renewed.

Research in psychology shows that positive reinforcement has a far stronger effect on behaviour and wellbeing than criticism. In fact, John Gottman's studies suggest that thriving couples maintain a 5:1 ratio of positive to negative interactions. Affirmation isn't about avoiding hard conversations; it's about ensuring that encouragement outweighs discouragement.

> Affirmation is truth spoken in love – never flattery, never manipulation

What Affirmation Looks Like

Affirming words can be simple yet powerful. They are often short phrases that acknowledge effort, character or presence.

Affirmation can:

- Notice effort – 'Thank you for picking up the groceries today.'
- Recognising qualities – 'I admire how patient you were with the kids.'
- Celebrating growth – 'I'm proud of how you handled that meeting.'
- Expressing value – 'I feel so grateful to share life with you.'

It doesn't always need to be grand or poetic. Affirmation can be spontaneous, but it can also be intentional. The more we affirm deliberately, the more natural it becomes. In fact, the most powerful affirmations are often the simplest, ***'I see you. I appreciate you.'***

When Affirmation is Missing

When affirming words are missing, a relationship doesn't just stagnate, it experiences a vacuum where connection should be. Partners begin to feel unseen, unappreciated or fundamentally undervalued. This quiet neglect gradually erodes intimacy and can breed resentment, cynicism or emotional withdrawal. The truth is that silence often wounds just as deeply as harsh words.

Cost of Unspoken Gratitude

Consider the story of Michael and Grace. Grace poured herself into keeping their household running smoothly, managing logistics and creating comfort. Michael rarely acknowledged any of it; he simply assumed she knew he was grateful. However, Grace's efforts began to feel less like expressions of love and more like thankless obligations. She felt invisible. When Michael finally began intentionally speaking the language of affirmation – 'I really value how you create such a welcoming home for us' – Grace's energy and outlook shifted entirely. The very same tasks that once felt draining now felt meaningful because her contribution was acknowledged and seen.

In Mark and Lani's case, after years of marriage Lani confessed, 'I know Mark loves me, but he rarely says it. I feel invisible.' Mark was genuinely shocked; he assumed his acts of service and presence spoke louder than words. Yet for Lani, unspoken love felt like unexpressed love. Mark's silence was interpreted not as neutrality, but as quiet disregard. He quickly learned that while his actions were appreciated, his relationship required the specific, intentional use of affirming words to truly register love and security with his wife.

The absence of this language sends a devastating, unintended message: You don't matter. To avoid this, we must actively choose to make our appreciation explicit and verbal.

> The smallest affirmations, spoken daily, build the strongest bonds

Common Barriers to Affirmation

Many people genuinely love their partners but still struggle to express affirmation consistently. The heart feels it, but the words never seem to make it out. Why?

- Upbringing: when praise wasn't the norm – for some, affirmation feels foreign because it wasn't modelled when they were growing up. In homes where love was shown through duty or correction rather than kind words, praise can feel awkward, unnecessary or even insincere. They may equate affirmation with flattery rather than encouragement.
- Assumption: they already know how I feel – it's easy to assume our partner already knows they're loved, valued or appreciated. But unspoken affection slowly loses its power. In truth, people rarely tire of being reminded that they matter. Love that is felt but never verbalised becomes invisible.
- Busyness: when life gets in the way – modern life is crowded with tasks, messages and mental noise. In the rush of work, parenting and routine, intentional affirmation can quietly disappear. Yet the moments that feel too busy for kind words are often the moments when they're most needed.
- Fear of dependence: I don't want them to rely on praise – some hold back affirmation out of fear that it will make their partner needy or complacent. But genuine affirmation isn't indulgence, it's nourishment. It strengthens confidence, not dependence. When given sincerely, it builds emotional security that allows both partners to grow.

Affirmation is not flattery. It is not manipulation. It is a form of honest recognition, rooted in truth and love. Where flattery exaggerates and manipulates to gain favour, affirmation highlights what is genuinely good, valuable or admirable in another. It does not seek to impress or control; rather, it builds trust by naming what is real.

For example, a husband might say to his wife, 'You're the most beautiful woman in the world, no one could ever compare to you.' While romantic, it can slip into flattery because it stretches beyond truth and may feel hollow over time. Contrast that with: 'I love the way your smile brightens the room; it always lifts my day.' That is affirmation – specific, grounded and true.

In another example, a wife might tell her husband, 'You're the smartest man alive, you always know everything.' That sounds like praise, but it is inflated and easily questioned. While affirmation would sound like: 'I admire how you handled that difficult conversation at work today, you stayed calm and thoughtful.' This speaks to observable reality, making it more powerful and believable.

Affirmation uplifts without distortion, reminding your partner that they are seen, respected and cherished for who they truly are. When practised consistently, it becomes a stabilising force in the relationship – not empty words, but a steady rhythm of truth-telling that reinforces love and strengthens connection.

> " Affirmation isnt about feeding egos, its about reminding the heart its seen

Reflection Exercise: Flattery or Affirmation?

1. Identify a phrase
   Think of one compliment you often give your partner. Write it down exactly as you usually say it.
2. Test it
   Ask yourself:
   - Is this rooted in truth (something real and observable)?

- o Is it specific (naming an action, trait or moment)?
- o Does it build connection rather than seek favour?

3. Reframe if needed
   If the phrase feels more like flattery ('You're always the best at everything'), rewrite it as an affirmation ('I really appreciated how you made time for me even when you were tired tonight').
4. Practise daily
   For the next week, aim to speak at least one honest affirmation to your partner each day. Keep it short, clear and grounded in reality.

Tip: Affirmations are strongest when they notice the 'small things' – everyday actions, attitudes or qualities that often go unremarked.

> " To affirm is to notice and name what is good and real in your partner

Science of Affirmation

The power of affirming words isn't just intuitive; it's verifiable through scientific research. Psychology and neuroscience confirm that affirmation plays a vital role in strengthening both individual wellbeing and the deepest bonds of a relationship.

Affirmation and the Brain

When we genuinely express or receive verbal appreciation, the reaction is biological. Studies have found that positive input activates the reward pathways in the brain, triggering the release of positive neurochemicals, such as dopamine and oxytocin. Dopamine is associated with pleasure and motivation, it reinforces positive behaviour. Oxytocin, the 'bonding hormone', deepens feelings of connection and trust. In essence, speaking affirmation literally generates joy and security in your partner's mind and in your shared connection.

Relational Bank Account

Beyond the neurological effect, consistent affirmation fundamentally changes the nature of a relationship. Research clearly shows that couples who express gratitude regularly report significantly higher relationship satisfaction and resilience. This is because small, consistent affirmations create what leading marriage researcher Dr. John Gottman calls an 'emotional bank account.'

Every sincere word of praise, thanks or appreciation is a deposit of goodwill. These deposits buffer the relationship against the inevitable withdrawals that occur during conflict or stress. When it's time to have a difficult conversation, a full emotional bank account ensures the couple approaches the discussion from a place of trust and warmth, rather than in fear and resentment.

In other words, affirmation is not just a 'nice to have' flourish in a relationship. It is a proven, necessary practice that provides the emotional nutrition required for long-term health, stability and growth.

> **//** Flattery inflates; affirmation grounds

Practical Ways to Practise Affirmation

Affirming words are most powerful when they are specific, sincere and steady. Learning to speak this language means moving beyond general compliments to making your appreciation an intentional, targeted part of your daily routine.

Focus on Specificity

The deepest affirmations are those that show your partner you are truly *seeing* them, not just making a generic comment.

- ♥ Be targeted: instead of a vague statement (like 'You're great'), strive for specificity ('I really admire the way you stayed calm and rational during that stressful call; that skill keeps us grounded'), which demonstrates that you were paying attention and value a specific quality or action.
- ♥ Affirm both being and doing: ensure your praise covers both your partner's character and their actions. Affirm who they are ('You are incredibly thoughtful') and what they do ('I appreciate how you took the initiative to fix that for us without being asked'). This provides a complete picture of their value.
- ♥ Catch the small things: don't wait for grand achievements or milestones. The strength of your connection is built on the mundane. Acknowledge and affirm the daily, often invisible, acts – the patience they showed, the meal they prepared or the way they listened to you vent.

Build Consistency and Rhythm

Affirmation should be a steady flow, not an occasional flood. Consistency creates the reliable emotional bank account that buffers a relationship against stress.

- ♥ Implement the Daily Three: commit to affirming your partner in three different ways each day: once about their character (who they are); once about their effort (what they did); and once about their presence (how they make you feel). This structured practice makes affirmation an unbreakable habit.
- ♥ Vary the channels: keep the language fresh and engaging by using different methods. Speak it aloud during conversation, write a thoughtful note on the mirror or send an unexpected message during a stressful workday. Variety ensures the affirmation always registers.

Amplify Impact

The setting or the audience can significantly multiply the power of an affirming word.

- ♥ Public praise: affirm your partner in front of others – your children, friends or family. Hearing you celebrate their qualities in public not only makes them feel incredible, but it also reinforces your loyalty and shared bond to the world.
- ♥ Use declarative language: use clear, declarative sentences that eliminate ambiguity. Phrases like 'I feel X when you do Y because Z' ensure your partner receives the compliment as a complete and sincere expression of your gratitude, rather than just a casual remark.

Daily Three Practice

For the next seven days, set aside a moment each evening to share three affirmations with your partner using the story of Elena and Victor as a guide. Make the session about:

- Who they are (qualities, character)
- What they've done (actions, efforts)
- What they mean to you (the relationship itself, presence).

Write them down if needed. At the end of the week, reflect on how this practice affected your emotional climate and share the list with your partner. Notice how both giving and receiving affirmation shifts the climate of your relationship.

Power of the Daily Three

Elena and Victor weren't fighting; they were doing something far more dangerous; they were drifting apart. After ten years of marriage and two children, their dialogue had become purely transactional.Their evenings were dominated by the tedious recital of schedules, chores and mounting logistics. They were excellent co-managers of a busy household but had forgotten how to be partners. The quiet space where affirmations once lived had been replaced by a weary silence. Victor felt his efforts were unacknowledged and Elena felt fundamentally unseen.

I introduced them to a powerful, deceptively simple tool: the Daily Three. The challenge was for each one to share three specific affirmations with the other every evening: one acknowledging their character, one about their effort and one celebrating their presence.

Initially, it felt intensely awkward and forced. Victor would stumble over a hesitant, 'I guess you're ... efficient', while Elena would mechanically reply, 'And you, umm, you got the shopping done'. They felt silly speaking about qualities they assumed the other already knew they appreciated.

Then, within two weeks, something shifted. Because they were actively and intentionally ***looking*** for things to affirm all day, they started ***noticing*** each other again.

One evening, Elena beamed: 'I look forward to hearing what Victor will notice about me each night. It's stopped being a duty and started feeling like a little gift.' Victor added, with genuine surprise in his voice, 'It's like we've discovered each other again. I'm seeing the qualities that made me fall for her, but I forgot to mention.'

The Daily Three didn't just change their words; it changed their relational climate. It replaced the transactional focus with emotional curiosity, proving that a consistent, small act of focused language can reverse the insidious process of two people quietly falling out of focus.

> " When you affirm what is true, love feels safe enough to grow

Reflection Questions

- When was the last time I felt truly affirmed by my partner?
- What kinds of affirmation mean the most to me – words about who I am or what I do?
- Do I find it easy or awkward to affirm my partner? Why?
- How often do I affirm my partner with words?
- What specific qualities in them do I admire but rarely articulate?
- How do I feel when I receive affirmation, and what does that reveal about my partner's need for it?

- ♥ If I affirmed my partner daily for one week, what difference might it make?

Closing Thought

Affirming words are not about flattery or denial; they are about vision – the deliberate choice to see the good in one another, even amid imperfection. They remind us that love is not sustained by grand gestures alone, but by small recognitions spoken often and sincerely.

When couples practise affirmation, they build a culture of *recognition rather than neglect*. They turn everyday moments into opportunities to say, 'You matter. I notice you. I'm glad you're here.'

In the rhythm of daily life, affirmation is the sunlight that keeps love alive – simple, powerful and freely given. It warms what has grown cold, strengthens what has become fragile and nourishes connection until it blooms again. Without it, love fades into assumption. With it, relationships flourish in safety and joy.

In essence, the language of recognition uses affirming words to say, 'I see you. I value you. I delight in you.'.

4. Empathic Words

> When you mirror feelings, you multiply trust

Why Empathy Matters

If Affirming words are the language of recognition, then Empathic words are the language of presence. Where affirmation says, 'I see you and I value you', empathy says, 'I feel with you. I am here with you in this moment.' They form two sides of the same essential coin: affirmation recognises your partner's qualities; empathy recognises their current experience.

Where affirming words celebrate and elevate, empathic words comfort and anchor. This language breaks the surface of achievement to meet your partner in the messier realities of life. It is the primary way partners feel truly understood in their struggles and genuinely safe in their vulnerability, clearly signalling: 'You are not alone in this. I am with you.'

Emotional Oxygen

Empathy is the emotional oxygen of a relationship. Without it, even the most deeply loving bond can begin to feel suffocating and restrictive. It is what allows us to breathe together through periods of tension, clears the fog of misunderstanding and soothes the quiet ache of feeling unseen. When empathy is present, it softens the air between us and acts as the emotional climate control that calms storms and restores safety.

While science tells us we are wired for empathy – our mirror neurons activate when we witness another's emotion, allowing us to organically resonate with their experience – it is never automatic. It is a skill. In a relationship, empathy is not instinctive, it is a choice. It's language changes emotional isolation to lasting emotional intimacy.

Radical Act of Feeling With

Empathy does not mean you have to fix the problem. Crucially, it doesn't even mean you have to agree with your partner's perspective or emotion. It means feeling with.

Empathy is the difficult, quiet courage of holding space for your partner's truth, even when that truth is different or challenging to your own reality. It is the radical act of saying, 'I may not fully understand this, but I want to. Tell me more.'

When empathic words flow freely, they become a source of profound security. They tell your partner that their internal world is a sanctuary, not a battlefield, and that you are committed to being a witness to their emotional life. In a world that constantly tells us to 'be strong' or 'move on', empathy gives permission to just be. It meets your partner in the middle of the mess – in disappointment, fear or confusion – and provides a safe emotional shelter. When spoken sincerely, empathic words communicate that you don't have to hold it all together right now. You're not a problem to solve, you're a person to love.

Empathy is the difference between *hearing* and *listening*, between *sympathy* and *understanding*. It transforms isolation into togetherness. In relationships, this kind of language becomes a bridge back to shared ground after stress or misunderstanding.

Through empathic words, couples learn that being 'strong' isn't about always being right or composed; it's about being real.

> " Empathy is not about fixing; its about feeling with

What Empathy Looks Like

Empathic words reflect understanding, compassion and shared feeling. They go beyond polite listening; they communicate, 'I am with you in this'. Empathic words do not rush to fix problems or to offer quick solutions, in fact, they intentionally resist that urge. Instead, they create space for a partner's feelings to be seen and acknowledged without judgement.

Speaking with empathy is about entering your partner's emotional world, naming what you observe and gently affirming its validity. It might sound like, 'that must have been really frustrating,' or 'I can see how much this matters to you.' In these moments, the goal is not to take away the feeling but to share it, to sit in it beside your partner. Such words communicate safety and presence by saying, 'I hear you. I get it. You're not alone in this.' In doing so, they forge connection at the deepest level, reminding both partners that emotions, even difficult ones, can be held together in love.

Examples include:

- ♥ 'That sounds really difficult. I can see why you're upset.'
- ♥ 'I'm listening, tell me more.'
- ♥ 'I imagine that must have felt frustrating when they ignored you.'

- 'That must be really hard for you.'
- 'I can see why you feel that way.'
- 'I may not fully understand, but I'm here with you.'
- 'It makes sense that you reacted like that.'
- 'I'm here with you. You don't have to go through this alone.'

Empathic words never minimise, dismiss or hurry emotions along. Instead, they create a safe space in which feelings can be expressed and held without judgement. But *how* you speak is just as important as *what* you say. A calm, gentle and attentive tone communicates care far more effectively than words spoken in haste or distraction.

EMPATHY AT WORK

One evening, Maya came home from work exhausted and frustrated. When she sighed heavily, her partner Kola looked up and asked, 'What's wrong now?' The words weren't cruel, but the rushed, irritated tone made Maya feel brushed aside.

Later that week, after learning about empathic words, Kola tried again. When Maya walked in looking drained, he softened his voice and said, 'It looks like today took a lot out of you. Do you want to talk or just rest for a bit?'

Maya described the difference clearly: 'It wasn't just the words. It was how he said them. I felt cared for instead of criticised.'

> Empathic words don't erase pain, but they make it bearable together

What Empathy Is *Not*

Many people confuse empathy with advice, sympathy or pity. But true empathy is:

- Not advice: empathy doesn't jump in with solutions ('You should have just said...')
- Not sympathy: sympathy can create distance ('Poor you'), while empathy closes the gap
- Not pity: pity looks down; empathy looks across, eye-to-eye.

At its heart, empathy is about presence. It's not about fixing your partner's feelings but about sharing them.

Dialogue: Empathic vs Non-Empathic

Take a scenario in which a partner comes home after a stressful day at work.

Non-Empathic Response (problem-fixing or dismissive)

- Partner A: 'I had such a rough day. My boss piled on more work, and I just feel exhausted.'
- Partner B: 'Well, maybe you should learn to manage your time better. Just don't let it get to you.'

This response minimises emotion and shifts straight into advice, leaving Partner A feeling unheard.

Empathic Response (presence and validation)

- Partner A: 'I had such a rough day. My boss piled on more work, and I just feel exhausted.'
- Partner B: 'That sounds really overwhelming. I can imagine how drained you must feel. Do you want to talk about it or just relax for now?'

This response acknowledges emotion, names it and offers companionship rather than a quick fix. Partner A feels validated and supported, even if the problem itself remains unsolved.

Barriers to Empathy

Why We Get Stuck

If empathy is the emotional oxygen of a relationship, why do so many couples struggle to let it flow freely? The difficulty arises because empathy requires us to temporarily set aside our own instincts – whether it's the urge to fix things, to defend ourselves or to look away from discomfort.

The most common barriers to the flow of empathic words fall into three categories:

1. Instinctual blocks – immediate, reflexive responses that shut down empathy before it can begin
    - Rush to fix (problem-solving mode) – we often mistake empathy for obligation and instead of offering pure presence, we immediately jump into problem-solving mode, dismissing the feeling with a swift 'Here's what you should do.' This invalidates the emotion because the partner simply wanted to be heard first
    - Discomfort with emotion – some people find strong feelings like grief, anger or anxiety deeply unsettling. This unease leads them to either withdraw entirely or to quickly shut down the emotion, often by minimising the partner's feeling or forcing a quick distraction
    - Emotional overload – when our partner's pain is significant, we can struggle to sit with it without feeling overwhelmed ourselves. This causes us to protect our own emotional capacity by prematurely

shutting down the conversation, a necessary boundary turned into an empathic failure.

2. Internal obstacles – these are internal states that prevent us from fully turning our attention toward our partner

    - Self-preoccupation (self-absorption) – when we are too consumed by our own worries, tasks or internal narratives, we simply lack the bandwidth to truly step into someone else's world. Empathy requires a quiet focus that cannot coexist with distraction
    - Defensiveness reflex – perhaps the most destructive barrier. When we hear our partner's pain (e.g. 'I felt hurt when you did X') as a criticism rather than an invitation to connect, our natural defence mechanism kicks in. We respond by justifying our actions or intentions, completely bypassing the opportunity to empathise with their hurt
    - Fear of blame: related to defensiveness, this fear makes us anxious about being judged. We worry that if we empathise with our partner's pain, it might be interpreted as an admission of fault, leading us to argue or stonewall instead of listening.

3. Environmental and cultural conditioning – the learned habits and societal norms that discourage emotional expression

    - Distraction and multitasking – in the modern world, many attempt to 'listen' while simultaneously scrolling, working or watching television. This partial presence is an instant empathy killer, signalling that the partner's feelings are less important
    - Cultural messages – for those who grew up in environments or cultures that equate emotional

expression with weakness or instability, the language of empathy can feel unfamiliar, awkward or even unsafe. This requires an intentional re-learning.

Learning to overcome these barriers is the key to mastering empathic words. Couples can then step back from their reactive instincts and choose empathy more intentionally, transforming a moment of tension into an opportunity for connection.

> Validation turns walls of defensiveness into doors of connection

Dialogue Examples

1. Partner looks upset after work
    - Less helpful: 'What's wrong now?' (rushed, dismissive)
    - Empathic: 'It looks like today was really draining. Do you want to talk about it or would you rather just relax?'
2. Partner seems quiet during dinner
    - Less helpful: 'Why are you being so moody?'
    - Empathic: 'You seem a little quiet tonight. Is something on your mind?'
3. Partner shares frustration about a friend
    - Less helpful: 'Well, maybe you're overreacting.'
    - Empathic: 'That sounds hurtful. I can see why you'd feel upset.'

Science of Empathy

Empathy is not just 'nice to have' in relationships, it is a measurable factor that predicts how satisfied couples feel and how long they stay connected. Research consistently shows that empathy is one of the strongest predictors of relationship satisfaction. In fact, studies in neuroscience reveal that when one partner expresses an emotion, the other partner's brain can literally begin to 'mirror' that emotion – a phenomenon called ***emotional contagion***. This mirroring explains why a sigh, a tear or a laugh can be so contagious. Our brains are wired to feel with those we love.

Psychologists have found that couples who practise empathy consistently build what is known as ***secure attachment***. This is the deep confidence that no matter what happens, 'my partner is with me.' Secure attachment is like the emotional anchor of a relationship: it keeps both partners steady in moments of stress, reduces anxiety when life feels uncertain, and allows for greater risk-taking and vulnerability within the relationship. When you know your partner will respond with empathy, you are more likely to share openly, lean on them for support and step into new challenges together.

Empathy also boosts resilience. Studies show that couples who regularly validate each other's emotions are better equipped to bounce back from conflict and stress. Empathic connection functions like an emotional 'buffer,' softening the blows of life's difficulties. Intimacy deepens because empathy reassures both partners that they are not facing their struggles alone. Over time, this creates a cycle of trust and closeness: the more empathy is practised, the more secure and intimate the bond becomes, which in turn makes empathy easier to give and receive.

> Empathy doesnt remove disagreement; it repositions partners on the same side

Shift from Fixing to Feeling

When James lost his job unexpectedly, he felt embarrassed, angry and worried about their finances. His first instinct was to withdraw, to avoid burdening his wife, Maria, with his feelings. But when he eventually told her, she didn't rush to offer solutions or remind him of their budget. Instead, she put her hand on his shoulder and said softly, 'I can see how heavy this feels for you. It must be scary to feel like the ground has shifted. But we'll face this together.' Those words – simple, empathic and grounded – became the turning point.

James later said it wasn't Maria's practical advice that carried him through that season, but her willingness to feel it with him.

Sophie came home exhausted, her shoulders heavy with the stress of a long day. Alex, wanting to help, immediately offered a solution, 'Maybe you should talk to your manager about it.' But Sophie didn't feel heard. What she needed wasn't advice, it was emotional presence.

Later that evening, after learning about empathic language, Alex tried something different. He looked at her gently and said, 'You sound completely drained. That must've been a lot to carry today.' Sophie exhaled. The tension softened. She felt seen, not analysed. Held, not handled.

That simple shift changed the atmosphere between them. Their evening unfolded with more closeness, less defensiveness. Alex realised something powerful: Sophie didn't need fixing, she needed feeling. And empathy, not solutions, was the bridge.

Healing Power of Empathy

David and Ngozi had been married for six years and arguments had become a regular part of their routine. David often felt attacked or criticised, while Ngozi felt as though her concerns were dismissed or brushed aside. Their conversations frequently spiralled into defensiveness and frustration, leaving both of them exhausted and disconnected.

When they began learning about empathic language, something subtle but powerful started to shift. One evening, during yet another disagreement about one of their children, David caught himself before reacting in his usual defensive tone. Instead, he took a breath and said, 'It sounds like you're hurt because you felt I didn't consider you when I made that decision about Anthony. That makes sense.'

For the first time, Ngozi didn't feel like her words were bouncing off a wall. Later she reflected, 'In that moment, I didn't feel like I was fighting you. I felt like you were standing with me, and we were both facing the problem together.'

It wasn't a magical fix, they still had disagreements, but the atmosphere changed.

Arguments no longer felt like battles to win; they became opportunities to listen, validate and understand. David and Ngozi discovered that empathy doesn't erase conflict, but it does transform it into a pathway back to connection.

> To listen with empathy is to say:
> you are not alone in this

Practical Exercises

Empathy is an accessible skill, not an innate talent, and it can be learned and mastered through consistent practice. The goal is to move from simply hearing your partner's words to truly entering their emotional world.

Phase 1: Create Intentional Presence

The first step in speaking empathic words is setting the scene. Empathy cannot coexist with distraction.

- **Create presence rituals**: before beginning a difficult or important conversation, intentionally remove barriers. Sit facing one another, make consistent eye contact and switch off any digital distractions. This ritual signals that 'my full attention is yours'
- **Listen before speaking**: commit to a single goal of focusing on hearing the feeling, not just the factual content. Resist the powerful, reactive urge to prepare your response while your partner is speaking.

Phase 2: Translate and Validate

Once you are present, use words that show your partner their experience has registered and is valued.

- **Reflect and name the emotion**: this is the core skill of empathy. Instead of just nodding, reflect back what you have heard, 'It sounds like you felt completely overlooked and frustrated when your manager missed that point.' By naming the emotion (frustration, sadness, anxiety), you offer a specific, validating label, confirming that you truly heard the emotional weight of their story

- **Normalise and validate the experience**: empathy does not require agreement, only validation. Even if you don't share their perspective, you can validate the feeling. Phrases like 'I understand why you feel that way' or 'anyone in your shoes would feel that kind of pressure' are incredibly powerful. They move the conversation past isolation and confirm the rightness of their emotional response.

Phase 3: Resist the Urge to Fix

True empathy is often about what you ***don't*** say and what you *ask* instead.

- **Stay present (don't solve)**: resist the impulse to instantly jump to solutions or advice. Empathy can require silence as much as it requires words. Your role is to hold the emotional space, not to instantly fill it
- **Ask, don't assume the need**: never assume you know what your partner needs in that moment, so ask a clarifying question: 'I hear how heavy that is for you. What do you need from me right now – just listening, or would you like me to offer some advice?' This honours their autonomy and ensures your presence meets their actual need.

By following these phases, you transform a potentially difficult exchange into a deliberate act of connection, making your relationship a reliable sanctuary during times of stress.

Empathy Pause

Next time your partner shares a difficult feeling, try this three-step process:

1. Pause – resist the urge to respond immediately with advice
2. Reflect – identify the emotion you hear ('It sounds like you felt ...')
3. Validate – offer presence ('I get why that upset you. I'm here').

Try this exercise three times in the next week and notice your partner's response. Take a breath, make eye contact and reflect back what you hear. Resist the urge to fix or explain. Afterward, ask whether that felt supportive.

> " Empathy is not about fixing;
> its about feeling with

Reflection Questions

- When my partner shares feelings, do I tend to listen, fix, dismiss, respond or empathise?
- How comfortable am I sitting with emotions, mine or my partner's?
- Which phrases could I practise this week to show more empathy?
- How do I usually show empathy, and how could I strengthen it?
- How might our relationship change if I slowed down to feel with my partner more often?

Closing Thought

Empathic words are like cool water in a desert; they refresh the spirit, soothe emotional exhaustion and create the necessary space for growth and healing to occur. While affirming words celebrate the good and build worth, empathic words bravely hold space for the difficult and the hard. Both languages are absolutely essential for a resilient connection.

Remember that practising empathy does not demand that you always agree with your partner's perspective, nor does it require you to absorb their pain as your own. That kind of emotional burden is unsustainable.

Instead, empathy is a profound and active choice to temporarily step into their world and stand there with them. It is the powerful, quiet commitment to never leave your partner to face their emotional struggles alone. This unwavering presence is, perhaps, the greatest gift you can give the person you love.

In essence, the language of presence uses empathic words to say, 'I am with you in this.'

5. Clear Words

Why Clarity Matters

Clear words are the language of safety. They say: 'This is what I mean, and this is what I need.'

Clarity is more than just good communication. It is emotional safety in action. It is the difference between guessing and knowing, between tension and trust. When we say, 'This is what I mean, and this is what I need,' we offer our partner a clear map through our emotional landscape. We stop asking them to read between the lines or to decode our silence.

Love is often assumed to be enough in relationships. But love without clarity can feel like walking through fog – confusing, frustrating and sometimes unintentionally hurtful. We may have the best intentions, but without clear words, those intentions get lost. That's when misunderstandings grow, when small missteps turn into big ruptures.

Clear communication doesn't mean being blunt or robotic, it means being emotionally honest. It means saying, 'I felt hurt when that happened,' instead of withdrawing and hoping they'll notice. It means asking, 'Can we talk about what just happened?' instead of quietly letting resentment build.

Clear words are the safe foundation to any resilient relationship. They are used to strip away ambiguity and passive resentment, ensuring both partners are working from an accurate map of their shared reality.

When we speak with clarity, we reduce the emotional guesswork. We give our partner the gift of knowing where they stand. And we give ourselves the gift of being understood.

As Brené Brown reminds us, 'Clear is kind. Unclear is unkind.' In love, clarity isn't just a skill, it's a kindness. A way of saying that I care enough to be understood and that I care enough to understand you.

When couples practise clarity, misunderstandings shrink and trust has room to grow. Without it, assumptions multiply, creating distance where there should be connection. Hints, half-truths and vague requests may seem easier in the moment, but they can leave both partners frustrated and second-guessing. Over time, this pattern of confusion slowly wears away intimacy, replacing openness with uncertainty.

Clarity is the opposite of relational fog. Where fog blurs vision and leaves couples stumbling in the dark, clarity illuminates the path ahead, making it easier to walk together with confidence. Think of clarity like a GPS for your relationship. Without clear directions, you may be moving, but you risk driving in endless circles or taking frustrating detours that lead to nowhere. Clear words let both partners know precisely where they are headed, how to get there and what wrong turns to avoid along the way. Clarity doesn't guarantee there won't be traffic or bumps on the road, but it ensures you're always travelling with the same map in hand.

When precision becomes a daily habit, intimacy is no longer clouded by uncertainty; it becomes brilliantly illuminated. The use of clear words teaches us the crucial skill of moving beyond what we *think* our partner knows, to stating exactly what we need them to hear to successfully participate in our life.

Problem with Guesswork

Without the safe language of clear words, partners are forced to operate on guesswork. They make assumptions about needs, interpret silent cues or rely on decades-old expectations that may no longer apply. This reliance on unspoken understanding is often the first crack in a relationship. It causes partners to miss the mark, not out of malice, but because they simply lack essential, current information.

When your words are clear – whether you are articulating a boundary, expressing a feeling or stating a simple need – you invite your partner to meet you in a space of safety and honesty.

> " Clarity is kindness: honesty spoken with care creates safety

Emotional Honesty: Courage to Be Real

Emotional honesty is the brave act of showing up in your relationship with your ***undistorted truth*** – without disguise, spin or damaging delay. It's the willingness to name what you feel, even when that feeling is messy, inconvenient or makes you feel incredibly vulnerable.

In the partnership dance, emotional honesty is the only reliable bridge between your inner experience and your shared understanding. Without it, partners are forced to guess, to interpret silence or – most dangerously – to fill in the emotional gaps with their own anxieties and fears.

Honesty Isn't Just Talking

Emotional honesty is not about uttering every unfiltered

thought that crosses your mind, nor is it a free pass to rage. It's about speaking from the heart with intention and care. It means expressing your needs, your boundaries and your feelings in ways that honour both yourself and the relationship's stability.

This is the key difference between 'I'm fine' (a polite lie that closes the door) and 'I'm feeling overwhelmed and I don't know how to ask for help' (a vulnerable truth that invites connection). That kind of truth is what truly creates emotional safety. It replaces guesswork with certainty. It invites closeness. It builds unwavering trust.

Risk and Reward

Why does this feel so difficult? Many of us were taught in childhood to suppress, soften or spin our feelings to avoid conflict or the dreaded fear of rejection. We internalise the belief that a 'perfect' partner is one without needs or strong emotions.

But when we hide our truth, we inevitably hide parts of ourselves. Over time, this quiet withholding erodes genuine intimacy. The most resilient couples aren't the ones who manage to avoid discomfort, they are the ones who courageously learn to navigate it, time and again, with transparency and care.

Emotional honesty is a daily practice. It asks us to tune in, slow down and choose clarity over comfort. It's not about being emotionally perfect, it's simply about being authentic. And authenticity is the only material that truly holds the structure of long-lasting love together.

What Clear Words Look Like

Clear words cut through fog. They remove guesswork and prevent misunderstanding by saying what needs to be said in a way that is both honest and kind. At their heart, clear words combine truth with respect, ensuring that communication builds trust rather than erodes it.

Clear Words are:

- ♥ **Direct** – they express the message without ambiguity. Instead of hinting, hoping or leaving your partner to read your mind, you say what you actually mean. For example: 'I'd love it if we could eat dinner together tonight' is far clearer than a vague 'You never want to spend time with me.'
- ♥ **Respectful** – they honour the other person while being honest. Clarity is not an excuse for bluntness or cruelty. Saying, 'I need more support around the house' is respectful; snapping, 'You're so lazy' is not. Respect frames truth in a way your partner can actually hear.
- ♥ **Simple** – they avoid overcomplication or hidden meanings. Clear words get to the point without long-winded explanations or loaded sarcasm. A simple, 'I'd like us to go to bed earlier together' is easier to understand – and act on – than a passive comment like, 'I guess some of us care about getting rest.'
- ♥ **Actionable** – they make it possible for the other person to respond. Saying, 'I feel overwhelmed when I do the dishes alone; could you help me with them after dinner?' invites action. By contrast, vague remarks like, 'This house is always a mess' only create defensiveness.

Clear Words are direct yet kind. They balance honesty with compassion. Clarity avoids blame-filled 'you always' or 'you never' statements, which often trigger defensiveness and shut down connection. Instead, clarity uses 'I feel' and 'I need,' which communicates responsibility and invites co-operation.

For example:

- ♥ Instead of: 'You never listen to me.'
  - Say: 'I feel hurt when I don't feel listened to. Could we take a moment to talk without distractions?'
- ♥ Instead of: 'You never help around the house.'
  - Say: 'Could you please wash the dishes tonight?'
- ♥ Instead of: 'I'm fine.' (when clearly not)
  - Say: 'I'm upset about what happened earlier. Can we talk about it?'
- ♥ Instead of: 'You don't love me anymore.'
  - Say: 'I feel disconnected lately and I'd like us to spend more quality time together.'

Clarity is not about demanding your way. It's about giving your partner a fair chance to understand you and about creating the safety of knowing where you truly stand. In a foggy world of mixed signals and hidden meanings, clear words are a gift – to your relationship, to your partner and to yourself.

> **"** Confusion erodes connection; clarity restores it

Clear Word Swaps

Table 5.1 Clear word swaps

Fog type		Clarity
Vague	'You should know what I need.'	'I feel overlooked when I have to carry this alone. I need help with the groceries this week.'
Critical	'You're so selfish.'	'I feel hurt when my needs aren't considered. Can we find a solution together?'
Generalising	'You never listen to me.'	'I feel unheard when I talk about my day and the TV is on. Could we turn it off while we talk?'
Passive	'It'd be nice if someone helped around here...'	'I'd appreciate it if you could take care of the dishes tonight so I can finish my work.'
Sarcastic	'Wow, thanks for showing up on time for once.'	'I felt frustrated waiting earlier. Could we agree on a time that works better for both of us?'
Blaming	'You're always on your phone.'	'I feel disconnected when we don't spend time talking. Could we set aside 20 minutes tonight just for us?'

Clarity is not about being harsh, it's about being honest in a way your partner can actually respond to. It replaces confusion with understanding and defensiveness with direction.

Couples Practice: 'Truth Exchange'

The purpose of this exercise is to create a safe space for each partner to share one honest feeling and one gentle request – without judgement, interruption or fixing.

1. Set the scene

    - Choose a quiet time when you both feel calm and open. Sit facing each other. No phones, no distractions. Just presence.

2. Take turns – each person completes the following two prompts aloud:
    - One honest feeling I've been holding: 'Something I've been feeling lately is ...' (e.g. disconnected, even though I know we're both trying)
    - One gentle request I'd like to make: 'Something that would help me feel more supported is ...' (e.g. a few minutes of undistracted time together each evening)
3. Listen without fixing – when your partner shares, simply listen. No interrupting, defending or problem-solving. Just receive. You can respond with:
    - 'Thank you for sharing that.'
    - 'I hear you.'
    - 'That makes sense.'
4. Reflect together – after you have both shared, take a moment to reflect.
    - What did you learn?
    - What surprised you?
    - What felt good?
5. Optional journal prompt – after the exchange, each partner can write
    - 'What did I learn about my partner's inner world today?'
    - 'What did I learn about my own?'

Anatomy of Clear Communication

Why We Avoid Clarity in Relationships

Clarity is kind, but it's not always easy. Here's why many couples struggle to speak clearly, even when they care deeply.

1. Fear of conflict: sometimes we avoid clarity because we're afraid it will spark an argument. We soften our words, speak in circles or stay silent altogether hoping to keep the peace. Ironically, vagueness often fuels greater conflict later. When needs go unspoken, they build up. When feelings are unclear, they get misinterpreted. Clarity may feel risky in the moment, but it's often the very thing that prevents an emotional explosion down the line.
    - Instead of: 'It's fine.'
    - Say: 'I felt hurt earlier and I want to talk about it calmly.'
2. Cultural habits: in some cultures, indirect communication is seen as polite or respectful. We learn to hint, imply or speak in code, especially around sensitive topics. But in intimate relationships, this can create confusion. What feels respectful in one context may feel evasive in another. Emotional safety thrives on clarity, not guesswork.
    - Instead of: 'You probably already know ...'
    - Say: 'I want to be clear about what I'm feeling, even if it's hard to say.'
3. Testing the partner: sometimes we drop hints or expect our partner to 'just know' what we need. It's a quiet test:

'If they really loved me, they'd figure it out.' But this sets both partners up for disappointment. Love isn't mind-reading, it's communication. When we speak clearly, we give our partner the chance to show up, not to fail a test they didn't know they were taking.

- Instead of: 'I shouldn't have to say it.'
- Say: 'Here's what I need right now – it would mean a lot.'

4. Emotional overload: in heated moments, clarity can feel impossible. Our words come out tangled – too sharp, too vague or too fast and less constructive. We speak from reactivity, not reflection. But emotional honesty doesn't require perfection. It asks for pause. For breath. For the courage to say, 'I'm overwhelmed and I want to speak clearly, but I need a moment.'

    - Instead of: 'You never listen!'
    - Say: 'I'm upset and I want to explain why without blaming.'

Without clarity, resentment grows and although silence may feel safe in the moment, it often costs more in the long run.

Cost of Unclear Words

Lack of clarity in communication creates emotional fog. Couples start navigating their relationship by ***guesswork*** rather than understanding. What isn't clearly said is quietly assumed, and those assumptions often drift far from the truth.

When meaning becomes murky, trust begins to wobble. Partners start reacting to what they ***think*** the other meant rather than what was actually said. Misunderstandings multiply and small moments of confusion slowly grow into deep feelings of disconnection.

Consider these common examples:

- When Emma told Ben, 'Do whatever you want,' he took her words at face value and assumed she was fine. In truth, she felt dismissed and unseen, hoping he'd notice her hurt without having to say it. Her vague words built a wall instead of a bridge.
- When Luis hinted that he was stressed but never explained what he needed, his partner Clara assumed he wanted solitude. What he actually longed for was closeness and comfort. The silence between the lines left both feeling misunderstood.

In both moments, love was present, but the language failed. Unclear words don't just confuse, they *disconnect*. Over time, emotional fog becomes emotional distance.

> " When words lose precision,
> relationships lose direction

From Hints to Honesty

Many couples don't mean to be unclear. They're simply trying to avoid conflict, protect feelings or test whether their partner is 'tuned in.' Yet, unspoken expectations create silent pressure and vague words invite misunderstanding.

Emotionally intelligent clarity doesn't mean harshness. It's not about speaking louder; it's about speaking *truer*. It is the courage to replace hints with honesty and to communicate needs directly, respectfully and warmly.

From Hinting to Speaking Clearly

Here are a few examples of how vague or indirect communication can be transformed into emotionally intelligent clarity.

Table 5.2 From hint to clarity

Hinting Language (Vague or Defensive)	**Emotionally Intelligent Rewrite (Clear and Caring)**
'Do whatever you want.'	'I'd rather we decide together, it matters to me.'
'It's fine.'	'I'm actually feeling disappointed, but I'd like to talk about it calmly.'
'I'm just tired.'	'I'm feeling emotionally drained and could use some time to rest or reconnect.'
'You should know what's wrong.'	'I'm upset about what happened earlier and I need to share how it felt.'
'Forget it.'	'I'm finding it hard to talk right now, but I don't want to leave it unresolved.'

Why Clear Words Heal

Clarity is love in plain language. It removes confusion before it becomes conflict and helps both partners respond to *what is real*, not to what is assumed. When couples learn to speak with both honesty and gentleness, they make understanding possible and safety inevitable.

In emotionally intelligent relationships, clarity is not cold; it's compassionate enough to say:

- 'I trust you enough to tell you the truth.'
- 'I believe we can handle honesty together.'

Reflection Practice

Think about a recent moment where you felt misunderstood. Ask yourself:

- Did I hint or did I express what I truly felt?
- What would a clearer, kinder version of that message sound like?
- How might clarity next time help us feel closer rather than conflicted?

> Honesty spoken with care doesnt cause distance, it creates direction

Practice Truth with Tenderness

1. Tune in – find a quiet moment. Close your eyes, breathe deeply and ask yourself:
   - What am I feeling right now?
   - Is there something I've been avoiding saying? Why?
2. Write it down – in your journal or workbook, complete the sentence 'If I were being emotionally honest today, I would say ...'
   - Let it flow. Don't edit. Just write what's true.
3. Choose your words with care – imagine sharing that truth with your partner.
   - Rewrite your sentence using emotionally intelligent language that honours both your truth and your connection
   - Example: Instead of 'You never listen to me', try 'I've been feeling unheard lately, and I really need to feel more connected when we talk.'
4. Share gently – when you're ready, share your truth in a calm moment.
   - Speak slowly
   - Let your partner respond
   - Stay open.

Science of Clarity

Clarity may feel like common sense, but research in communication studies shows that it is a critical factor in relationship health.

Studies consistently reveal that when partners communicate with clarity – directly expressing their needs, feelings and expectations– they report lower stress levels, fewer conflicts and higher levels of satisfaction. In fact, clear communication has been linked with stronger problem-solving, more effective conflict resolution and greater trust between partners.

Why does clarity matter so much? Because the human brain is wired to close gaps in information. When something feels uncertain or incomplete, we instinctively fill in the blanks – and often with negative assumptions. If your partner withdraws without explanation, you might assume they are angry. If they give a vague response to your concern, you might conclude that they don't care. This tendency, sometimes called ***negative attribution bias***, means that unclear communication fuels anxiety and misunderstanding.

Clarity acts as an antidote. By putting feelings and needs into clear words – 'I'm tired and need some quiet tonight' or 'It hurt me when that was overlooked' – couples remove the guesswork that breeds tension.

Research shows that partners who practise clarity are more likely to have their needs met, precisely because those needs are named. This builds a positive cycle: clarity increases understanding > understanding fosters responsiveness > responsiveness strengthens trust.

Clarity also reduces the emotional load on a relationship. Without it, partners expend energy decoding each other's intentions, tone or silence. With it, energy is freed for deeper intimacy, problem-solving and joy. In other words, clarity is not just about communication; it is about efficiency in love. It clears away the noise so that couples can focus on what really matters – being present with one another.

Ultimately, clarity transforms relationships because it transforms safety. When couples know they can speak and be heard directly, they no longer walk on eggshells or worry about misinterpretation. Instead, they build a foundation of honesty and trust that can carry them through both everyday life and the hardest of storms.

From Hints to Clarity

For years, Amara would drop hints when she wanted help around the house. She might sigh loudly while folding laundry or mutter, 'I guess I'll do the dishes, again.' Her husband, Tunde, often missed these cues. He thought she was just venting, not asking for help, and he carried on with what he was doing. This left Amara feeling ignored and resentful, while Tunde grew frustrated, insisting, 'I can't read your mind!'

When they began to learn about the role of clarity in communication, Amara tried something new. Instead of hinting, she looked at Tunde and said, 'I'm feeling overwhelmed with the housework tonight. Could you please wash the dishes so I can finish the laundry?' Tunde immediately agreed. He wasn't unwilling to help, he just hadn't known she needed him in that moment.

Later, Amara admitted that speaking directly felt vulnerable at first, but it also felt liberating. For the first time in years, she wasn't left wondering why her needs were unmet. Tunde reflected, 'When you're clear with me, it's so much easier to show up for you. I don't have to guess.'

This simple shift – from hints to clarity – reduced their stress and built new trust. By naming her needs openly, Amara created space for Tunde to respond with love.

From Guessing to Knowing

Naomi often felt frustrated with her husband, Chris. She wanted more help at home but never asked directly. Instead, she sighed loudly or made indirect comments: 'The laundry never ends around here.' Chris didn't respond, assuming she was just venting.

Finally, Naomi tried a clear approach: 'Chris, could you take responsibility for folding the laundry twice a week?' To her surprise, Chris agreed. What she had expected to be a fight became a simple conversation.

Naomi reflected, 'I realised I'd been punishing him for not reading my mind. Clear words changed everything.'

> Clear words don't wound; they heal uncertainty

From Fog to Clarity

Table 5.3 Emotional rewrites for real-life moments

Fog	Emotional Impact	Clarity Rewrite	Reflection Prompt
'I'm fine'	Leaves the partner guessing; creates emotional distance and tension	'I'm feeling overwhelmed and not ready to talk yet, but I will when I've had a moment'	When do I say 'I'm fine' to avoid deeper truths? What would it feel like to name what's underneath?
'You should already know'	Feels like a test; breeds resentment and disappointment	'I realise I haven't said this clearly, I need more reassurance when I'm feeling insecure'	Have I expected my partner to read my mind? What's one need I can express more clearly?
'Whatever. Do what you want'	Sounds passive-aggressive; signals withdrawal or emotional hurt	'I feel unheard right now, and I need a moment before we decide together'	When do I use dismissive language to protect myself? What would it take to speak with vulnerability?

Fog	Emotional Impact	Clarity Rewrite	Reflection Prompt
'You always do this' or 'You do this all the time'	Feels like blame; escalates conflict and shuts down listening	'When that happened, I felt dismissed. Can we talk about it calmly?'	Do I use absolutes when I'm hurt? How can I name my feelings without attacking?
Silence after conflict	Creates uncertainty; feels like emotional abandonment	'I'm still processing what happened. I care about us and want to talk when I'm ready'	When do I go quiet instead of expressing my truth? What helps me feel safe enough to speak?
'You're too sensitive'	Invalidates feelings; erodes emotional safety	'I didn't realise that landed so harshly. Can you help me understand how it felt?'	Have I dismissed my partner's emotions? How can I respond with empathy instead of defensiveness?

Relief of Honesty

Mark always dreaded asking his wife, Leila, about weekend plans. She often said, 'I don't mind, you choose', only to seem annoyed later with his choice. One evening, he gently asked, 'Leila, what do you really want to do?' She hesitated, then admitted, 'I'd love to just stay in and watch a film.'

Mark laughed and said, 'That's all I needed to know.' They both felt relieved. Leila later said, 'I realised I'd been hiding what I wanted, thinking it would make me easier to love. But clear words actually made things easier for both of us.'

> " When love is clear, trust has room to breathe

Bridge and Wall of Dialogue

The ability of a couple in an emotional fog to restore safety, hinges largely on their use of clear language to express their feelings about the situation that created the conflict. A useful concept to navigate this is what I call the Bridge and the Wall of Dialogue.

Invariably, every conversation between a couple, especially one that is taking place when an emotional fog has cast a gloom over the relationship, is an opportunity to build one of two things: a ***bridge*** or a *wall*. Both are constructed by words, but they serve opposite purposes.

A Bridge of Dialogue (constructive) is built using emotionally intelligent languages that connect partners. It's a structure of trust and understanding, made piece by piece through empathy, clarity and genuine concern. When you use affirming, empathic, clear, repairing, curious and visionary words, you build a way over the inevitable chasms of misunderstanding and disagreement. The goal is not to win an argument, but to foster a deeper connection and work together toward a shared solution. It brings you closer, even when the conflict seems solid.

In contrast, the Wall of Dialogue (destructive) is a defensive barrier, constructed with words that push your partner away. It's built using blame, criticism, sarcasm, contempt and defensiveness. Instead of seeking to understand, this type of dialogue seeks to protect yourself, to assign fault and to shut down meaningful conversation. Every hurtful accusation, every snide comment and every refusal to listen adds another stone to this wall, making it taller and thicker, until you can no longer see your partner.

Recognising whether your words are building a bridge (constructive) or a wall (destructive) is a critical step in transforming your communication patterns. The examples that follow will help you see these two forms of dialogue in action and will equip you with the tools to consistently choose the path of connection.

Figure 5.1 Bridge and wall of dialogue

Messy House

Few issues spark tension in couples quite like simple household chores. In many relationships, a 'messy house' quickly stops being about dirt and becomes a symbol of far deeper frustrations: concerns about fairness; unspoken resentment over responsibility; or the feeling of being chronically taken for granted.

Manifesting as destructive dialogue, blame inevitably takes centre stage: 'You never clean up after yourself!' or 'You always leave everything for me to deal with!' These infamous 'you always/never' statements are verbal hand grenades. They escalate conflict immediately because they attack the partner's character, leaving one person feeling defensive and the other unheard and frustrated. Constructive dialogue, powered by clear words, immediately shifts the focus.

By using 'I' statements and naming a specific, observable need, couples transform frustration into a solvable problem. For example, replacing attack with request: 'I feel overwhelmed when the kitchen is left messy. Could we agree on a plan to share the cleaning this week?'

The difference is subtle, yet profoundly powerful. Blame pushes partners apart and closes the door to listening, while clarity invites co-operation and opens the door to partnership. Clarity allows the couple to negotiate a shared reality rather than fight over individual resentments.

Table 5.4 Destructive to constructive dialogue

	Destructive Dialogue	Constructive Dialogue
Alex	'This house is a disaster. You never help me clean up! I'm always the one picking up your mess.'	'Hey, can we talk for a minute? I'm feeling overwhelmed with how messy the house is right now.'
Morgan	'That's not fair! I was busy all day, and besides, you're the one who leaves dishes in the sink.'	'I know, I'm sorry. I had a rough day.'
Alex	'Oh, so now it's my fault? You're just so lazy. You have never cared about our space ever.'	'I get that. I'm feeling a little stressed and it would really help me if we could tackle this together. What can we do to get it under control?'
Morgan	'Fine, I guess I'll just live in a pigsty then. It's not worth fighting about – is it?' (walks away)	'You're right. Let's make a plan. I'll take care of the kitchen and the living room if you handle the bedroom. How does that sound?'

Unanswered Texts

This scenario focuses on how assumptions and emotional reactions can escalate a small issue. The clear dialogue addresses the feeling first, before jumping to conclusions.

Table 5.5 Destructive to constructive texts

Name	Destructive Texts	Constructive Texts
Jane	'I can't believe you didn't text me back for hours. You must have been out with friends as usual. You always do this.'	'Hey. I was trying to get in touch with you earlier and I didn't hear back. It made me feel a little worried. Is everything okay?'
Taylor	'What are you talking about? I was in a meeting. Why do you automatically assume the worst in every situation?'	'Oh, I'm so sorry! I was in a meeting that ran late and had my phone on silent. I should have let you know as soon as I could.'
Jane	'Because you don't care about me, that's why. If you did, you would have found a way to let me know.'	'I appreciate that. It's just sometimes when I don't hear from you, my mind goes to some bad places.'
Taylor	'This is ridiculous. I'm not going to sit here and be accused of things I didn't do.' (storms out)	'I understand. I'll make sure to text you even if it's just to say I'm in a meeting. I want you to feel secure.'

Forgotten Plans

This scenario shows how to handle disappointment and express needs without it degenerating into a personal attack.

Table 5.6 Destructive to constructive disappointment

Name	Destructive Disappointment	Constructive Disappointment
Tobi	'Are you kidding me? You forgot we were supposed to have dinner with my parents tonight? You are so selfish. You never remember what's important to me.'	'I'm feeling really hurt right now because I thought we were having dinner with my parents tonight. It was important to me, and I was looking forward to it.'
Lara	'It completely slipped my mind! I'm so busy with work. Why do you always have to make such a big deal out of everything? I'm so feed up of all these.'	'Oh, no! You're right, I completely forgot. I am so, so sorry. I know how much this means to you.'
Tobi	'A big deal? This isn't just about dinner. This is about you not valuing my family.'	'Thank you for acknowledging that. It means a lot. Can we still find a way to make it work, or can we reschedule for a night this week?'

Name	Destructive Disappointment	Constructive Disappointment
Lara	'That's a lie! Stop attacking me.'	'Let's call them right now and reschedule. I will put it on my calendar with a reminder. I promise it won't happen again.'

Practical Exercise

Ways to Practise Clear Words

- State needs, not just feelings – 'I feel tired, and I need some help with dinner.'
- Use 'I' statements – 'I feel ...' instead of 'you always ...'
- Be specific – replace vague requests with concrete ones. Change 'help me more' to 'please cook dinner on Tuesdays.'
- Check understanding – ask, 'can you please tell me what you heard me say?'
- Avoid mixed messages – don't say 'it's fine' if it isn't.
- Ask for clarity – if your partner is vague, gently ask, 'can you please tell me more about what you mean?'
- Pair clarity with kindness – direct words don't need harsh delivery. Don't say 'I just have to tell it as it is.'

Reflection Questions

- Do I tend to speak clearly, or do I expect my partner to guess?
- What is one area where my partner often misunderstands me?

- How could clarity reduce tension in our relationship this week?
- How often do I expect my partner to 'just know' what I need without saying it?
- What fears hold me back from being clearer in my communication?
- When was the last time clarity resolved something that vagueness had made worse?

> Clarity makes space for intimacy to flourish

Closing Thought

Clear words are not harsh; they are kind. They may feel risky, but vagueness is riskier. They remove the fog of assumption and create a path of trust. They allow partners to truly know one another, not guess or assume.

Clear words create safety and understanding, allowing partners to meet one another's needs without confusion.

In essence, the language of safety uses clear words to say, 'This is where I stand, and this is what I need.'

6. Repairing Words

> Forgiveness is the weld of marriage

Why Repair Matters

Repairing words are the language of healing that carry the humility to say, 'I was wrong. I'm sorry. Let's restore what was broken.' No matter how deeply two people love one another, conflict is unavoidable. Stress, fatigue, differing perspectives and unmet expectations all create friction. What separates thriving couples from struggling ones is not the absence of conflict, but the presence of repair.

Psychologist John Gottman, whose research on marriage spans decades, notes that successful couples are not those who argue less, but those who repair more effectively. Conflict is inevitable; contempt, silence or defensiveness is not. Repairing words interrupt the cycle of hurt and prevent it from hardening into resentment.

Repairing words are not about winning or losing. They are not about minimising, explaining away or justifying an action. They are about recognising the reality of hurt, taking responsibility and communicating the desire to reconnect. They sound like: 'I see that what I said was harsh. I shouldn't have spoken that way. Can we try again?' or 'I know I let you down and I want to make it right.' Such words close the gap conflict creates and remind both partners that their bond is stronger than any disagreement.

Without repair, wounds linger. Small offences accumulate like stones in a backpack, growing heavier over time until the relationship feels burdened and distant. Unrepaired hurts breed bitterness, mistrust and emotional withdrawal. However, with repair even painful conflicts can become opportunities for growth. Apology and forgiveness are not signs of weakness but acts of courage, signalling: 'Our connection matters more than my pride.'

Couples who practise repair develop resilience. Each time they work through a disagreement, they emerge not only reconnected but also more confident in their ability to handle future conflicts together. Repair becomes the bridge that turns a stumbling block into a stepping stone to deeper trust, safety and intimacy.

What Repairing Words Look Like

Repairing words emerge from a place of humility, accountability and a desire for restoration. They are those essential phrases – including genuine apologies, heartfelt acknowledgements, active forgiveness and intentional invitations to rebuild – that stop conflict from spiralling and allow couples to successfully mend their connection after a disagreement or hurt.

Repair is not an act of weakness; it is an act of profound courage. It signals that you value the health and future of your relationship above your own need to be right, to defend your intentions or to avoid temporary discomfort.

Four Components of Relational Repair

Repairing words work by using specific, intentional language to rebuild the bridge of trust and are:

1. Genuine apology (accountability) that goes beyond a simple 'sorry' and takes ownership of the impact on your partner
    - Example: 'I was wrong. I'm sorry for how I spoke to you – it was disrespectful, and I take full responsibility for my tone.'
2. Heartfelt acknowledgement (validation) of your partner's experience and pain, even if you still disagree with the facts of the argument
    - Example: 'I see clearly how my actions hurt you. That wasn't my intention, but the impact was real, and I am sorry you felt that pain.'
3. Invitation to rebuild (forward motion) as an active reaching out to re-establish connection and move out of the emotional rut
    - Example: 'Can we start again? I want to reconnect now or at least agree on a time when we can.'
4. Active forgiveness (release), choosing to release the debt of the past and to focus on the future
    - Example: 'I forgive you. I'm letting that go now, and I'm ready to move forward together.'

Repair is not magic; it is medicine. It does not possess the power to erase past hurt, but it absolutely can and must heal the sting. The goal of repairing words is to transform a painful memory from open wound to respected scar, a proof of resilience.

This language is the vital mechanism that prevents past injuries from being weaponised in the present. By successfully engaging in repair, you ensure that every conflict, rupture or mistake becomes a profound lesson in rebuilding and deepening the bond. Without effective repair, every future disagreement will inevitably drag up the relationship's entire history, making genuine resolution impossible.

When you master repairing words – through timely apologies, genuine accountability and active forgiveness – you create a safe psychological container in which vulnerability and imperfection are allowed. This gives both partners the confidence to be authentic, knowing that the foundation is strong enough to handle the inevitable cracks and is always mendable.

Repair cannot rewrite history, but it can redeem it. It turns pain into wisdom, mistakes into movement and wounds into ways back to one another. It is love's way of saying, 'The past may have hurt us, but it will not define us.'

> " Every couple argues; what matters most is how they repair

Why We Resist Repair

If repair is so vital, why do so many couples avoid it?

- ♥ Pride – it feels easier to defend oneself than admit fault
- ♥ Fear of rejection – what if my partner doesn't forgive me?
- ♥ Blame-shifting – 'I'll apologise if they do first'
- ♥ Minimising – 'it wasn't that big of a deal'
- ♥ Skill gap – many people simply don't know how to apologise effectively.

The absence of repair is never neutral; it is quietly corrosive. Silence after conflict doesn't heal, it hides the wound while it deepens. What remains unspoken doesn't fade with time; it festers in the dark and, left unattended, small fractures widen. What could have been healed through honesty becomes layered with misunderstanding and resentment. In time, the silence speaks louder than the original wound.

Science of Repair

Conflict in relationships is not only inevitable, it is also normal. What determines whether couples thrive or struggle is not the number of arguments they have, but how they handle them. Relationship researchers John and Julie Gottman, known for their decades of work on couple dynamics, emphasise the crucial role of ***repair attempts*** – those moments where one partner tries to soften tension, de-escalate conflict and restore connection.

The Gottman's research has shown something remarkable: couples who repair successfully are far more likely to stay together, regardless of how much conflict exists in their relationship. In other words, high-conflict couples who learn to repair can be just as stable and satisfied as low-conflict couples, because it is not the ***presence of disagreement*** that predicts success, but the ***presence of repair***.

Repair does not have to be polished, poetic or perfectly timed. Even clumsy repair attempts make a measurable difference. A partner blurting out 'Okay, let's not fight, I love you' or reaching for a hand mid-argument may feel awkward, but it signals a desire to reconnect. The intent matters more than the delivery. Such gestures interrupt the downward spiral of escalation and remind both partners that the relationship is more important than winning the argument.

Studies also reveal that repair works best when couples have built what Gottman calls a 'culture of positivity.' This means that small, consistent deposits of kindness, humour and affection in daily life make it easier for repair attempts to succeed during conflict. A gentle joke, a smile or a softening phrase – 'I know we're upset, but I don't want us to hurt each other' – can act as powerful repair tools.

Repair is not a one-time fix but a habit. Each attempt to close the gap after conflict sends a message: 'Our connection matters. I value us more than my pride or my point.' Over time, this creates resilience in the relationship. Couples begin to trust not that conflict will vanish, but that it will always be survivable. And that trust, built one repair at a time, becomes one of the strongest predictors of lasting love.

> It is not the presence of disagreement that predicts success, but the presence of repair

Examples of Repair Attempts

Repair attempts can be verbal or non-verbal. They don't need to be eloquent; they just need to signal 'I want us to reconnect'.

Verbal

- 'I don't like how this is going; can we pause and start over?'
- 'I'm sorry, I shouldn't have said that.'
- 'Let's take a breath. I love you, and I don't want us to fight like this.'
- 'I see your point; can we find a middle ground?'
- 'I know we're both upset, but I'm on your side.'

Non-Verbal

- Reaching out to hold your partner's hand mid-argument
- Using humour gently to break tension (a playful smile or light comment)
- Softening your tone and lowering your voice
- Offering a hug or physical closeness after raised voices

- ♥ Taking a short break to calm down, then returning with warmth.

Remember: Repair doesn't erase the conflict, but it stops the spiral and reopens the door to connection.

> A sincere apology is not weakness, but the courage to rebuild trust

Victim Mentality Impact on Emotional Repair

The reality is that every relationship has moments of hurt: words that wound; disappointments that linger; times when one partner feels unseen or unloved. But, over time, if that hurt becomes the lens through which everything else is viewed, it can evolve into something far more complex: a victim mentality.

Victim mentality is not a matter of being hurt. It is not a character flaw. It is a subconscious defence mechanism that the individual uses to protect themselves from the terrifying prospect of shame or accountability. By assigning all blame externally, the individual preserves the image of a 'blameless self', but in doing so, they dismantle the couple's capacity to heal.

A victim mentality can quietly but profoundly block a couple's ability to restore trust, communicate constructively and practise emotionally intelligent language. It's when a person identifies with their hurt. Instead of seeing pain as something to process, they begin to see it as part of who they are, while taking a morally superior stance in conflict.

Victim mentality isn't the same as being a victim of wrongdoing. Real pain, betrayal or neglect are all valid experiences. The problem begins when those experiences harden into an identity; when the person moves from saying 'I was hurt' to 'I am always the one who is hurt.'

In this mindset, the focus subtly shifts from healing to justification. Pain becomes a kind of emotional proof – a shield against accountability and, sometimes, against vulnerability. In relationships, this mindset can subtly but powerfully erode the foundation of emotional growth, sabotaging relational repair and being a defensive armour that inhibits the effectiveness of the six languages.

How Victim Thinking Manifests

The victim stance often begins as self-protection (based on real experiences of disappointment, betrayal or neglect). It feels safer to hold on to injury than to risk being hurt again. But what starts as protection can become imprisonment by distorting how a person interprets every interaction. While the pain is valid, the ***position*** becomes rigid. The person becomes trapped in the role of the wronged one, which makes growth and repair difficult.

It's characterised by thoughts such as:

- 'You don't understand how much I've suffered.'
- 'You're the one who always causes pain.'
- 'It's not my fault; I just react to what you do.'

In conversations, this looks like:

- Recounting past events in great detail but resisting any acknowledgment of personal contribution
- Seeking apology but never offering it
- Measuring every present moment against an unresolved past.

This creates an emotional imbalance between couples trying to repair. One partner is living in the past, while the other is pleading for a future. The relationship becomes a courtroom (full of evidence, verdicts and emotional sentencing) rather than a home.

How Victim Mentality Disrupts Repair

Repairing words require mutual vulnerability and self-awareness, empathy and responsibility. Each partner needs to say, 'We both matter. We both have a part in the healing.' Victim mentality blocks that process and creates an emotional imbalance because it traps one person in the role of the ***wronged*** and the other in the role of the ***perpetual offender.*** A situation in which one partner seeks acknowledgment but resists accountability.

Let's see how this mindset disrupts each of the six emotionally intelligent languages using Table 6.1.

Table 6.1 Effect of victim mentality

Language	Healthy Expression	When Victim Mentality Interferes
Affirming words	'I appreciate what you've done to make things right'	The victim partner struggles to affirm the other, seeing themselves as the only one deserving validation
Empathic words	'I can imagine how hard that was for you too'	By focusing on their own hurt, the victim leaves little space for the other's emotions
Clear words	'This is what I need, and this is how we can move forward'	Communication keeps circling back to the past, avoiding clarity about present needs
Repairing words	'I take responsibility; I'm sorry'	The victim stance resists ownership as apology feels like surrendering moral ground
Curious words	'Help me understand how we got here'	Curiosity gives way to defensiveness, questions feel threatening rather than enlightening

Language	Healthy Expression	When Victim Mentality Interferes
Visionary words	'Let's create a new chapter together'	Vision feels unsafe; holding on to grievance feels safer than risking hope

When pain becomes a person's identity, every effort at reconciliation is filtered through suspicion. No matter what the other partner says, it's never enough because the goal is no longer repair; it is validation of a distorted moral superiority.

Emotional Logic

It's important to remember that victim mentality is not always conscious. At its root, victim mentality is an *emotional defence*, often grounded in a deep fear that 'If I stop being the one who was hurt, will my pain still matter?'

Holding on to injury can feel like the only way to ensure it isn't forgotten. Unfortunately, this emotional logic backfires as the person stays tethered to the very wound they want healed. Love requires reciprocity, giving and receiving compassion, responsibility and repair, but this means that the person with the victim mentality can't fully receive love.

The tragedy is that clinging to pain blocks connection. It feels safe, but it isolates. This emotional stance creates what therapists call a *power imbalance of innocence*: one partner claims the moral high ground while the other carries a perpetual blame. That dynamic kills curiosity and trust, and turns repair attempts into further evidence of failure.

Here is how a victim mentality systematically sabotages use of the six emotionally intelligent languages.

Sabotaging Affirming Words

- Victim mentality: 'Your praise is manipulative or simply irrelevant.'

- Effect: Affirmation, noticing, encouraging and appreciating is rejected. The compliment is dismissed as 'too little, too late' or as an attempt to distract from the deeper 'injustice.' Positive observation is filtered out because it contradicts the core identity of being a suffering, unrecognised figure within the relationship.

Sabotaging Empathic Words

- Victim mentality: 'You must feel my pain, but I am not responsible for yours.'
- Effect: The person demands constant validation and empathy for their own hardship but refuses to offer it in return. They use shared painful experiences to reinforce the narrative of blame, turning empathy into a one-way transaction. True empathy (feeling with the partner) is blocked because it requires them to step out of their assigned role as the wronged party.

Sabotaging Repairing Words

- Victim mentality: 'The past is my proof, and your apology is insufficient.'
- Effect: The victim mindset weaponises the past by constantly recounting old events. This ensures the partner can never complete the three Rs of repairing words (recognise, remorse, restore; see Chapter 2). The apology is rejected because accepting it means the crisis ends and the victim loses their moral high ground, their only perceived source of safety.

Sabotaging Clear Words

- Victim mentality: 'You should know what I need without me asking.'
- Effect: A victim script prevents the direct, respectful expression of need. Instead of using clear words, they

use passive-aggressive communication (pouting, hinting or martyrdom). This forces the partner to guess and invariably fail, which reinforces the victim's belief that they are fundamentally misunderstood and mistreated.

Sabotaging Curious Words

- Victim mentality: 'I already know what you're going to do.'
- Effect: Curiosity requires openness to the partner's present reality and future possibilities. The victim mindset is rigidly closed, viewing the partner through the lens of past failures. This extinguishes exploration and rediscovery because they are certain they already know the unhappy ending, thus pre-emptively protecting themselves from future disappointment.

Sabotaging Visionary Words

- Victim mentality: 'We can only move forward if you perfectly fix the mistakes of the past.'
- Effect: The future is held hostage by the past. The shared vision becomes entirely conditional. Planning and dreaming together stops being an act of co-creation and becomes a transaction based on the partner's compliance with the victim's demands for retribution or retroactive justice. The relationship cannot progress with shared purpose.

Breaking the Cycle

The first step to shifting victim mentality is self-differentiation – helping the person separate ***what happened to me*** from ***who I am now***. Instead of saying, 'You hurt me, so I can't trust you,' the reframed thought becomes, 'I can't change what happened, but I can shape what happens next.'

Empathy from the other partner can help, but it must be balanced with gentle accountability, without which empathy becomes enablement. Encouraging statements might sound like:

- 'I see how much this has hurt you, and I also see how much you long for healing. What would moving forward look like for you?'
- 'We've both made mistakes; what would help you feel safer to rebuild rather than revisit?'

That shift from helplessness to ownership transforms communication. It invites both partners back to emotional equality, where empathy can flow in both directions. Practical ways to begin this shift include:

- Replacing 'You hurt me' with 'Here's how I felt when that happened.'
- Replacing 'You've never changed' with 'Here's what would help me feel safe moving forward.'
- Replacing 'I can't forgive you' with 'I'm still healing, but I'm open to rebuilding trust.'

Each reframe moves from accusation to agency, from being stuck in the story to rewriting it together.

Why It Matters for Restoration

Victim mentality keeps couples stuck in an emotional yesteryear – revisiting old injuries rather than repairing them – but true empathy listens to pain and true accountability honours growth. In healthy relationships, these two work hand in hand. If one partner offers empathy but the other refuses accountability, the relationship stagnates. If one demands accountability but offers no empathy, the relationship becomes punitive.

Healing happens only when both partners can hold two

truths at once:

1. 'Yes, I was hurt.'
2. 'I also have the power to help heal this.'

That shift from victimhood to agency reopens every emotionally intelligent language. Affirmation returns. Empathy flows in both directions. Repair feels possible again. And the relationship begins to breathe.

> Forgiveness is loves way of writing a new chapter

Practice: From Victim to Voice

The goal of this exercise is not to deny pain but to reclaim the power to respond differently. When we shift from a *victim mindset* ('This always happens to me') to an *empowered voice* ('Here's what I need to move forward'), healing becomes possible and emotionally intelligent language can flow again.

Use Table 6.2 to practise turning reactive or self-defensive thoughts into constructive communication.

Table 6.2 From victim to empowerment

Victim-Focused Thought	Underlying Emotion	Reframed, Empowered Thought	Emotionally Intelligent Response
'You never understand what I've been through'	Loneliness, frustration	'I want to feel more understood when we talk about the past'	'Can I share what that experience still means to me and then hear your side too?'

Victim-Focused Thought	Underlying Emotion	Reframed, Empowered Thought	Emotionally Intelligent Response
'It's always me trying to fix things'	Resentment, exhaustion	'I feel tired of being the only one initiating repair'	'I'd really appreciate it if we could both share the responsibility for rebuilding trust'
'You ruined everything between us'	Betrayal, anger	'Our relationship has been deeply hurt, but I still want to heal it'	'I know we've both made mistakes, can we talk about what change would look like for each of us?'
'You don't deserve my forgiveness'	Pain, fear	'I'm still hurting, and forgiveness feels hard right now'	'I'm not ready to let go yet, but I want to understand what forgiveness could look like over time'
'I can't move on until you admit everything'	Control, fear of dismissal	'I need acknowledgment to help me rebuild trust'	'When you acknowledge what happened, it helps me feel safe enough to start trusting again'

Use Table 6.2 to reflect on:

- ♥ Which statements do I relate to most and what do they reveal about what I fear losing or protecting?
- ♥ How do I tend to speak when I feel powerless or unseen?
- ♥ What might change if I replaced accusation with honest expression of need?

This framework shows that the six languages are not simply habits; they are states of vulnerability and shared accountability. The victim mindset, which prioritises self-protection above all else, makes true relational transformation impossible until that core script is rewritten.

> Your voice becomes healing when it speaks from ownership, not from injury

Anatomy of a Good Apology

Not all apologies are equal. A genuine repair goes beyond 'sorry' and contains five key elements:

- Acknowledgement – name what you did, 'I snapped at you unfairly'
- Responsibility – own it without excuses, 'That was my fault'
- Empathy – recognise the impact, 'I see how that hurt you'
- Commitment – express a desire to do better, 'I'll work on pausing before I speak'
- Invitation – ask for reconnection, 'Can we move forward together?'

Without these, apologies can fall flat. 'I'm sorry you feel that way' is not an apology, it's a deflection, and excuses or half-apologies often cause more harm than silence.

> Repair is the art of turning fractures into stronger bonds

Apology – Gift to the Injured Partner

An apology is a powerful first step in repairing a rift in your relationship. It's an act of courage and empathy from the person who caused the hurt, a way of acknowledging the pain they inflicted. An effective apology is not about justifying actions or demanding an immediate absolution. Instead, it is a gift offered to your partner – a clear statement of responsibility, a validation of their feelings and an expression of remorse. It's an invitation to begin the slow and often difficult process of healing.

Forgiveness – Gift to Yourself

Instead of viewing forgiveness as a reward to be earned, it's healthier to see it as a gift to yourself. This is arguably the most challenging part of the emotional repair process. Forgiveness is a deeply personal journey of releasing the resentment, anger and hurt caused by an offence. It is an act of letting go, not to excuse the other person's actions, but to free yourself from the emotional burden of carrying the weight of the past. The goal of this process isn't to forget what happened or to instantly absolve your partner, but to liberate your heart and mind so that both of you can move forward and rebuild.

Repair = Apology and Forgiveness

Repair is incomplete without forgiveness. Forgiveness is not forgetting or excusing; it is releasing the hold of resentment. It says, 'I choose to move forward with you.'

Couples who practise forgiveness experience greater resilience. They learn that mistakes are not fatal; they can be bridges back to one another.

Apology as an Act of Strength

Many people view apologising as a loss, a surrender in the battle of who is right. In truth, a sincere apology is an act of strength. It requires self-awareness, humility and the courage to admit imperfection. When one partner says, 'I was wrong and I'm sorry', it lowers defensiveness and creates space for healing.

Research shows that apologies are most effective when they name the offence, express regret and communicate a desire to change. Far from weakening a person, they demonstrate maturity and commitment to the relationship.

Forgiveness as a Choice to Heal

Forgiveness is the weld of marriage, although it is often misunderstood as forgetting or excusing hurtful behaviour. In reality, forgiveness is a deliberate choice to release resentment and open the door to reconciliation. It does not erase the wrong, but it does prevent the wrong from poisoning the relationship further. Forgiveness says, 'I choose our connection over holding on to anger.'

The belief that the severity of the offence should correlate with the time it takes to forgive is a transactional view of relationships. This perspective can lead to:

- ♥ Conditional forgiveness, which makes forgiveness a price that the offender must earn through an indefinite period of penance
- ♥ Power imbalance, when the wronged person withholds forgiveness to exert control over their partner
- ♥ Stagnation of healing, as the relationship gets stuck in a cycle of repeated apologies and unresolved hurt – the victim remains in a state of suffering, and the offender remains in a state of shame – instead of moving forward.

The myth that there is a timeline for forgiveness is a common misconception that can lead to unhealthy phases of shame and control, but couples who practise forgiveness report higher levels of satisfaction because forgiveness creates emotional safety, allowing love to breathe again after conflict.

A heart that's planted in forgiveness doesn't dwell in the past.

Why Pride Blocks Repair

Pride insists on being right. It clings to the illusion of control, making repair nearly impossible. Pride whispers, 'If I apologise, I lose. If I forgive, I look weak.' But in relationships, this mindset only breeds distance.

Repair requires both partners to see that the relationship itself is the priority. By letting go of pride, couples say, 'We win together or we lose together.' This shift in perspective transforms conflict into an opportunity to strengthen trust.

Repair as a Signal of Value

Every apology and every act of forgiveness carries a powerful message: 'Our connection matters more than my pride.' When couples consistently signal this to each other, they establish a foundation of security. Partners feel reassured that the relationship is resilient and that no disagreement, no mistake, is bigger than the bond they share. This reassurance turns conflict from a threat to stability into an opportunity for intimacy.

Courage to Begin Again

Repair is not about erasing the past; it is about creating a new beginning after a rupture. It takes courage to say, 'let's start afresh,' especially when hurt has run deep. But every time couples take that step, they reinforce the belief that their love is worth protecting. The courage to begin again transforms repair from a mere response into a practice that, over time, builds resilience, trust and enduring intimacy.

> Every apology and every act of forgiveness carries a powerful message

Barriers to Forgiveness

Forgiveness is often misunderstood. It is not:

- Denying the hurt, 'It didn't matter'
- Excusing bad behaviour, 'That's just who they are'
- Rushing healing, 'I forgave you, so let's pretend it never happened.'

Forgiveness is a process begun by repairing words, but rebuilding trust may take time and courage, however, it pays dividends in love.

Couple Who Learned to Repair

Angela and Marcus often argued over parenting decisions. Their fights escalated quickly, with both saying harsh things they regretted. For years, they avoided repairing, each waiting for the other to make the first move.

In counselling, they learned to practise repairing words. Marcus tried first: 'Angela, I was harsh last night. I criticised you instead of listening. I'm sorry.'

Angela softened. She replied, 'I know I raised my voice too. Thank you for apologising. I forgive you.'

That simple exchange became a turning point. They say, 'Repairing words saved our marriage.'

Practical Exercises

Practising Repair Through Apology and Forgiveness

The purpose of this exercise is to help couples experience repair as an act of courage and reconnection, not of weakness.

1. Identify the hurt
   - Each partner takes a moment to reflect on a recent disagreement or moment of hurt
   - Write it down briefly in one or two sentences – example, 'I felt dismissed when you looked at your phone while I was sharing about my day.'
2. Speak the apology (Partner A) – apologies should include three key parts
   - Naming the hurt ('I realise I hurt you when I ….')
   - Expressing regret ('I'm sorry for the way that made you feel.')
   - Commitment to change ('Next time, I'll put my phone aside, so you have my full attention.')

Tip: Avoid words like 'but' or excuses, they weaken the apology.

---

3. Offer forgiveness (Partner B) – which can be expressed through such words as
   - 'I accept your apology and I forgive you'
   - 'I was hurt, but I choose our connection over my anger'

- 'I want us to move forward together'

Note: Forgiveness is a choice, not a feeling. Sometimes the feelings take longer to heal, but forgiveness starts the process.

---

4. Switch roles so that both partners can practise giving and receiving repair
5. Reflect together and discuss these questions:
   - How did it feel to apologise directly?
   - How did it feel to forgive?
   - What made the process easier?
   - What felt challenging?

> Forgiveness is a process initiated by repairing words

Practical Ways to Practise Repairing Words

- Apologise early – don't let wounds fester
- Use 'I' statements – own your part, 'I was wrong' not 'We both messed up'
- Offer reassurance – remind your partner of your commitment
- Create rituals of repair – a hug after a disagreement, a phrase that signals peace
- Forgive freely – when your partner repairs sincerely, receive it with grace.

'Start Again' Ritual

I read about Jorge and Mei who developed a simple ritual of repair. Whenever conflict left them disconnected, one would say, 'Start again?' The other would respond with a nod or a smile. It became their shorthand for repair.

Mei explained, 'It doesn't erase what happened, but it reminds us that our love is bigger than the fight. It's a way of saying, "We're on the same team".'

Forgiveness Breakthrough

Aaron and Sophie were on the brink of separation. After years of unresolved arguments, their marriage felt like a house of locked doors. Conversations ended in silence, never in repair. Both carried hurts that had piled up over time. Small dismissals, harsh words and unmet needs had gradually built a wall between them.

One evening, after yet another disagreement that left Sophie in tears, Aaron realised the pattern had to change. Instead of withdrawing into silence, as he usually did, he tried something different. Taking a deep breath, he said quietly, 'I was wrong to shut you out. I see how it hurt you. I want to do better.'

The words were simple, even clumsy, but they carried a weight Sophie hadn't felt in years. She broke down and wept – not only from the pain of the past, but also from the relief of finally feeling seen. That moment didn't erase the years of hurt, nor did it magically solve all their problems. But it cracked open the door that had long been closed.

Sophie reflected, 'That was the first moment I believed we could find our way back.' Forgiveness began to take root not because the past was forgotten, but because Aaron's words showed humility and a willingness to repair.

This is the breakthrough of forgiveness: it doesn't rewrite history, but it reopens the future. It creates a pathway for healing to begin and for trust to be slowly rebuilt. For Aaron and Sophie, that first step was enough to turn despair into possibility. It showed that forgiveness, even when fragile, has the power to breathe new life into a relationship.

Lessons from Aaron and Sophie

1. Small words can carry great weight
   Forgiveness doesn't always begin with eloquent speeches. Aaron's simple apology – 'I was wrong to shut you out' – was enough to soften years of distance. What matters most is sincerity, not perfection
2. Repair opens doors, it doesn't erase the past
   Sophie's tears weren't a sign that the pain had vanished, but that she felt seen. Forgiveness is less about wiping the slate clean and more about choosing to walk through a reopened door together
3. Humility is stronger than pride
   Pride builds walls; humility builds bridges. Aaron's willingness to admit fault shifted the dynamic from having become adversaries to being partners again
4. Forgiveness makes the future possible
   Couples don't have to agree on every detail of the past to begin again. Forgiveness allows partners to invest energy in building a new future instead of reliving old hurts.

> " Repair doesnt erase the past;
> it reweaves it with grace

Reflection Questions

- When I recount past hurts, am I seeking understanding or re-establishing my innocence?
- What would it mean to let go of the story that keeps me 'right' but disconnected?
- How might taking a small responsibility actually make me feel stronger, not weaker?

> " Healing begins the moment we trade the need to be right for the courage to be real

Closing Thought

Repairing words are the ultimate proof that your love is stronger than your mistakes. The goal is never perfection; it is humility and the courage to acknowledge the gap you helped create. Their use reminds us that hurt is not the destination, but a temporary stumbling block on a shared path.

Repair is not about magically erasing the mistake, but about the profound, mutual act of renewing trust. Every timely apology, every honest act of accountability, and every courageous offer of forgiveness is a step in the active process of building resilience.

Remember: forgiveness is a gift to yourself, not a reward you reluctantly hand to your partner.

In essence, the language of healing uses repairing words to send the clearest signal of all: we've inevitably stumbled and caused pain, but we choose to stand together, mend the breach and move forward.

7. Curious Words

Why Curiosity Matters

Curious Words are the language of discovery to signal: 'I want to know you more, and I know you are worth the effort.' The power of this language is perhaps most transformative in moments of tension. Curiosity acts as a powerful softener of defensiveness.

Curiosity is, without doubt, one of the most underrated forms of love. In the effervescent early stages of a relationship, it flows naturally. Questions tumble out, stories are eagerly shared and every glance feels like a doorway to something new: 'What truly lights you up?'; 'What are you afraid of losing?'; 'What's your earliest memory of feeling safe?' In those moments, we aren't just gathering biographical facts, we are actively building the foundation of emotional intimacy.

The challenge is that familiarity can become a form of blindness. We start to make the dangerous assumption that we know our partner completely and that there is no new territory to explore. Intentional questions fade and new stories go untold. Slowly, the relationship shifts from being a thrilling discovery expedition to being a predictable, sometimes tedious, routine.

This shift doesn't happen because love is gone, but because curiosity ceased showing up. When we stop asking questions, we stop inviting our partner to be fully seen.

Curiosity is the emotional security blanket that keeps love

alive. It is the language that makes your partner feel intensely valued by confirming: 'I still believe you are fascinating.' This is crucial because no one stays the same. We constantly grow, change our dreams, carry new wounds and face new challenges. When genuine curiosity is present, we grow together instead of apart.

In a conflict, instinctive, reactive words sound like an accusation: 'Why are you like this?' or 'You're doing that again.'

However, curious words shift the emotional landscape by replacing accusation with invitation: 'Can you help me understand what that situation felt like for you?' That deliberate shift from demanding an answer to requesting context creates immediate emotional safety. It is the difference between conflict that damages and conflict that becomes a moment of deeper, more compassionate connection.

Curiosity isn't just a charming trait at the beginning of love – it is an indispensable skill required throughout a resilient, long-lasting partnership. It is how we commit to perpetually rediscovering each other.

What Curious Words Look Like

Curious words are open-ended, engaging and invitational. They create space for discovery rather than shutting down conversations. Unlike interrogations, which can feel like a cross-examination, curious words are rooted in genuine interest. They don't demand answers; they invite sharing. When spoken with warmth and attentiveness, they communicate: 'I want to know you better. Your thoughts and feelings matter to me.'

Curious words transform ordinary conversations into opportunities for connection. Instead of asking, 'Did you do that?' in a suspicious tone, curiosity reframes it as, 'Can you tell me how that went for you?' Instead of, 'What were you thinking when that happened?', which can sound accusatory, curiosity sounds like, 'Help me understand what you were thinking when that happened.'

After years together, it is tempting to believe you know everything about your partner, but that assumption – that closing down of knowledge – is the slow death of intimacy.

When couples practise curious words, they deliberately step out of the trap of assumption and into the freedom of shared exploration. They use an active language that honours the fundamental reality of partnership: people grow, they change, and their inner world is a universe that can only be uncovered when someone cares enough to ask.

Curiosity is love's way of saying: 'You are still a mystery worth discovering, even after all these years.'

By choosing to explore with a genuine interest, you prevent a victim mentality from taking hold. You transform conversations from transactional exchanges (logistics, tasks, to-do lists) into meaningful, relationship-building encounters.

Art of the Open Question

The essence of this language lies in asking questions that focus not on facts, but on feelings, experiences and dreams. Curious words should be delivered with sincerity, where your body language and attention match your spoken invitation.

1. Explore the inner world: these questions validate your partner's current state and historical reality; they signal that you care about the internal landscape they inhabit, not just the role they play in your life
    - 'What's been on your mind lately?'

- 'How did that make you feel?'
- 'How did you feel about that conversation with your friend?'
- 'What's one thing you wish I understood better about you?'

2. Look ahead and grow together: curiosity is also the fuel of a shared future and these questions ensure you remain aligned on purpose and passion, preventing the drift that happens when partners stop dreaming together

   - 'What are you looking forward to right now?'
   - 'What's something you'd love for us to try together this year?'
   - 'What's something new you're reading or learning about right now?'

3. Deepen vulnerability: the highest level of curiosity invites safe, unprecedented sharing in which you gently explore the hidden corners of relationship history or personal past

   - 'What's something you feel you've never fully told me before?'

When asked with sincerity, these questions do not pry but open. They nurture a relationship culture in which both partners feel seen, valued and, most importantly, continually rediscovered. Curious words create space for new insights and forge a deep, sustained connection built on continuous learning, not static knowledge.

> " Curiosity says: I am still learning about you, even after all these years

Reflection Prompts

- When was the last time I asked my partner a question just to know them better?
- What assumptions have I made about who they are or how they feel?
- What's one thing I'm curious about in their inner world?
- How do I respond when they ask about me, do I open up or shut down?

Questions That Keep Love Alive

Because love isn't just felt – it's discovered again and again.

Discovery Questions

For staying curious about each other's inner world

- What's something you've been thinking about lately but haven't said out loud?
- What's one part of your story I don't know yet?
- What's a dream you've quietly held on to?
- What's something that made you feel deeply seen in the past?

Intimacy Questions

For deepening emotional closeness

- When do you feel most emotionally safe with me?
- What's something I do that makes you feel truly loved?
- What's a fear you've never fully named in our relationship?
- What helps you open up when you're feeling guarded?

Playfulness Questions

For keeping joy and laughter alive

- What's the silliest memory we've shared that still makes you smile?
- If we could drop everything and go anywhere tomorrow, where would we go?
- What's a quirky habit of mine you secretly adore?
- What's a spontaneous thing you'd love us to try together?

Growth Questions

For aligning values and future vision

- What do you imagine our life looking like in five years?
- What's something new you'd love us to learn or explore together?
- What kind of legacy do you want our relationship to leave?
- What's one way we've grown as a couple that makes you proud?

Repair and Reflection Questions

For navigating conflict and building resilience

- What's something I could do differently when we disagree?
- When was a time we repaired well after a rupture? What helped?
- What's one thing you wish I understood better about you?
- How do you feel when I apologise? What makes it land well?

Difference Between Curiosity and Interrogation

Not all questions show curiosity. Tone and intent matter.

In emotionally intelligent relationships, the goal isn't just to ask questions, it's to ask them with love and openness, with the intent to connect, not to correct. Because when we lead with curiosity, we create space for truth. And truth, spoken in safety, is what keeps love alive. A question can open a door or shut it. It can invite closeness or trigger defensiveness. The difference often lies not in the words themselves, but in the tone and the intent behind them.

Consider these two examples:

- 'I'd love to hear how that meeting went for you.'
- 'Why didn't you do what I suggested in that meeting?'

Both are questions. But only one feels safe. The first expresses interest, care and emotional presence (curiosity). The second conveys judgement, control or frustration (interrogation). When tone shifts from curiosity to interrogation, the emotional climate also shifts. Instead of feeling valued, the listener feels cornered.

Curiosity is a form of emotional generosity that says, 'I want to understand you.' Interrogation, on the other hand, often masks fear, disappointment or unmet expectations. It says, 'I want you to explain yourself,' and that subtle shift can make all the difference.

Curiosity invites openness. Interrogation provokes defensiveness. The key is the heart behind the question – is it driven by love and interest, or by control and judgement?

> Questions open doors that assumptions keep shut

Barriers to Curiosity

If the language of discovery uses curious words, why do so many couples choose the state of idling over using them? The truth is that intentional curiosity requires effort, focus and a willingness to confront discomfort. The most common blocks to discovery fall into three categories:

1. Assumption Trap

This is the greatest long-term threat to intimacy.

- Assumption blindness: we stop asking questions because we convince ourselves that we already know everything about our partner. This mindset freezes them in history, missing out on the new dreams, challenges and lessons they are absorbing every day. Unspoken assumptions create emotional distance, as our partner senses we are no longer interested in their evolving reality
- Fear of answers: curiosity is inherently vulnerable, as it carries the risk of hearing something unexpected. We may avoid asking deeper questions because we fear the answer, perhaps a change in their goals, a resentment they carry or a need we feel unqualified to meet. This aversion to difficult truth replaces genuine connection with a comfortable, but ultimately fragile, silence.

2. Tyranny of the Immediate

Modern life is designed to consume attention, leaving little bandwidth for intentional connection.

- Chronic busyness: life's relentless demands – work deadlines, parenting, household maintenance – leave little mental space for deeper, meaning-making conversations. We default to clear words (logistics) but find we have no emotional reserves left for curious words. The relationship is managed efficiently, but intimacy stagnates.
- Technological distraction: the ever-present glow of phones, screens and background noise crowds out the space vital for real dialogue. Trying to initiate a curious question while multitasking signals to your partner that they only have part of your attention, killing the vulnerability required for an honest answer.

3. Self-Referential Hearing (Ego Filter)

This is the habit of listening to your partner only through the filter of how their words reflect on you. Instead of hearing their experience, you are preoccupied with defending yourself or pre-planning your rebuttal. This is a critical component of the victim mentality.

- Erosion mechanism: replaces sincerity with defensiveness. The moment your partner says anything that could be interpreted as a slight or a criticism, your curiosity is obliterated by your need for self-protection. When this happens, you stop asking to understand and start asking to accuse or deflect.

To master curious words, a couple must constantly work to dismantle these three internal barriers, allowing them to truly see, hear and accept their partner as they are.

Ultimately, it is a significant mistake to treat curiosity as optional. It is not merely a charming quality of new love; it is essential fuel for long-term intimacy, ensuring your commitment grows alongside the ever-changing person you married. Without it, even the strongest foundation begins to crumble under routine.

> Love isnt just felt – its discovered, again and again

Curiosity Prompts for Couples

Use these open-ended questions to spark discovery and deepen connection. They work in everyday conversations, date nights or even during quiet moments at home.

Daily Life and Feelings

- 'What was the best part of your day today?'
- 'What's been weighing on your mind lately?'
- 'How are you really feeling about this week?'

Dreams and Hopes

- 'What's something you're looking forward to in the next few months?'
- 'If time and money weren't obstacles, what would you love us to do together?'
- 'What's a dream you haven't shared with me yet?'

Memories and Reflections

- 'What's a childhood memory that shaped you?'
- 'What do you remember most vividly about when we first met?'
- 'Who has influenced you most in life, and how?'

Growth and Discovery

- 'What's something new you'd like to learn or try?'

- 'In what ways do you feel you've changed in the past year?'
- 'What helps you feel most supported by me?'

Tip: Ask with genuine curiosity, not as a checklist. Listen attentively, reflect back what you hear and let the conversation unfold naturally.

Science of Curiosity in Relationships

Curiosity is not just a pleasant trait, it is also a powerful driver of relational health.

Psychological research shows that curiosity is consistently linked to greater satisfaction, intimacy and resilience in couples. Partners who keep exploring – who continue to ask questions and show interest in each other's inner worlds – report higher closeness and lower boredom than those who assume they already 'know everything' about their partner.

Curiosity nurtures what psychologists describe as *self-expansion* – the process of growing together through shared experiences and discoveries. When one partner tries a new hobby, explores a new idea or pursues a fresh challenge, curiosity allows the other to join that journey instead of standing apart. Over time, this creates a sense that the relationship itself is expanding, keeping it vibrant and dynamic rather than stagnant.

Neuroscience provides another fascinating insight: curiosity activates the brain's reward pathways, releasing dopamine – the same chemical associated with motivation, pleasure and learning. This means that curious conversations are not only more engaging in the moment but they also strengthen the brain's association between your partner and positive emotional rewards. In simple terms, when we stay curious, our partner becomes more rewarding to interact with.

Curiosity also builds resilience. Couples who practise curiosity rather than making assumptions are better equipped to navigate change, because curiosity helps them adapt instead of resist. Asking, 'How are you experiencing this?' or 'What does this mean for you?' during transitions – whether moving house, becoming parents or facing loss – creates space for understanding, reduces defensiveness and increases the sense of being 'in it together.'

In everyday life, curiosity can be the difference between distance and discovery. A partner who chooses to ask, 'What excites you most about this project?' rather than simply nodding in silence, communicates interest and investment. Over months and years, these small moments accumulate into a powerful message: 'You are still worth knowing, and I never want to stop learning about you.'

> Love stays alive when discovery never stops

Rediscovering Through Curiosity

After 10 years of marriage, Luke and Mary felt as though their conversations had grown stale. Most evenings were filled with routine check-ins ('How was your day?') followed by brief, practical answers. Each one felt a distance growing between them, although neither knew how to reduce it.

One weekend, while on a long drive, Mary decided to try something different. Instead of the usual small talk, she asked, 'If you could go back to school and study anything, what would it be?' Luke paused, surprised by the question. Slowly, he began sharing his teenage fascination with architecture, a dream he had quietly set aside.

That one question sparked a deeper conversation that lasted the entire journey. Luke spoke about how creativity still mattered to him, and Mary began to see her husband through fresh eyes. Later she said, 'I realised there was so much about him I'd stopped asking about, so much still to discover.'

From that day, they began weaving curiosity back into their daily rhythm, asking each other open-ended questions that invited reflections, dreams and stories. Their relationship didn't transform overnight, but it gradually became lighter, warmer and more alive. For Luke and Mary, curiosity wasn't about novelty, it was about rediscovery.

When Curiosity Fades

Paul and Hannah had been married for 12 years. Their conversations revolved around schedules, bills and parenting. One day, Hannah admitted, 'I miss when we used to just talk.'

They began a simple weekly practice of asking each other three curious questions, such as, 'What's something new you'd love to learn?' or 'What was a highlight of your week?'

Within months, their connection deepened. Hannah said, 'It feels like we're dating again, but better.'

A Question that Changed the Evening

During dinner, Lorna asked her husband, 'What's one thing you wish I asked you more often?' He paused, then said, 'I wish you'd ask how I'm really doing, not just how my day went.' That simple question opened a conversation that night which was deeper than any they had shared in months.

> " Curiosity protects against the boredom of familiarity

Practical Ways to Practise Curious Words

- Ask open-ended questions – invite more than a yes/no answer
- Stay present – show genuine interest, not distracted listening
- Follow up – don't just ask; explore the answers
- Be playful – curiosity isn't just serious; it can spark laughter and fun
- Set aside time – create 'curiosity nights' with no agenda but to ask and listen
- Explore the past – ask about childhood memories or forgotten experiences
- Explore dreams together – ask about hopes, goals and future possibilities.

Curiosity Jar

A weekly invitation to explore each other's inner worlds.

The gap between knowing how to and actually being curious is often bridged by ritual. This simple, playful exercise guarantees that discovery remains a consistent, non-pressured part of your relationship rhythm.

Preparation

Together with your partner, find a jar, box or bowl – something that feels special. Decorate it if you like. Make it yours. On slips of paper, write down 20–30 open-ended questions that spark reflection, storytelling or imagination – focusing on inner life, feelings and dreams.

Ritual

Set a non-negotiable time each week, perhaps over a cuppa on Sunday morning or after dinner, to pull out one slip. Each partner answers the question fully, focusing only on listening and understanding. Let the conversation flow. No rushing. No fixing. Just presence.

This simple ritual keeps curiosity alive. It ensures that crucial, non-transactional conversations get scheduled, guaranteeing that you are continually growing ***toward*** each other, not merely parallel to one another. It turns ordinary evenings into moments of emotional intimacy. It reminds you that your partner is still becoming, and so are you.

Mood Menu

The Curiosity Jar Mood Menu is a gentle invitation to explore each other's inner worlds, one question at a time. It's a themed guide to help you choose questions that match how you're feeling that day or week. Whether you're craving laughter, depth, intimacy or repair, the menu helps you stay emotionally attuned while keeping curiosity alive.

In long-term relationships, it's easy to assume we already know everything about our partner. But people evolve. Desires shift. Stories deepen. The Mood Menu reminds us that there's always more to discover – if we're willing to ask, listen and stay open. This matters because it:

- ♥ Keeps connection fresh – you'll uncover new layers of each other, even after years together
- ♥ Builds emotional safety – choosing a theme together creates shared intention and reduces pressure

- ♥ Supports emotional regulation – some days call for lightness, others for depth; the menu meets you where you are
- ♥ Strengthens communication – these questions model emotionally intelligent language and invite meaningful dialogue
- ♥ Creates a ritual of presence – it's not just about the questions, it's also about slowing down and truly seeing each other.

Themed Question Sets

Choose your theme based on how you feel this week. Let your mood guide your connection, then:

- ♥ Set aside 20–30 minutes once a week
- ♥ Take turns asking and answering one or two questions from any listed in the below themes
- ♥ Listen without interrupting or defending
- ♥ After each answer, respond with empathy or affirmation – not advice.

1. Emotional depth, for when you want to connect beneath the surface and are craving real talk and heart-to-heart honesty
    - o What's something you've never said out loud but often feel?
    - o When do you feel most emotionally safe with me?
    - o What's a wound from your past that can still echo?
    - o What helps you feel truly understood?
    - o What's a part of yourself you're still learning to love?
2. Playful and light-hearted, for when you want to laugh, imagine and enjoy each other's quirks

- o If we could teleport anywhere for dinner tonight, where would we go?
- o What's a silly habit you secretly love about me?
- o If our relationship were a movie, what genre would it be?
- o What's your dream lazy Sunday?
- o What's a childhood snack you wish still existed?

3. Growth and dreams, for when you're feeling reflective or future focused

    - o What's something you'd love us to learn or try together?
    - o If you could design our ideal year, what would it include?
    - o What's a personal goal you're working toward – and how can I support you?
    - o What kind of legacy do you hope we'll leave as a couple?
    - o What's one thing you hope never changes between us?

4. Love and intimacy, for deepening emotional and physical closeness

    - o What's one way I make you feel loved?
    - o What's a moment when you felt most connected to me?
    - o What's something you'd love more of in our intimacy?
    - o What does emotional closeness mean to you?
    - o What's a small gesture that makes a big impact for you?

5. Conflict and repair, for when you're rebuilding trust or navigating tension

- o What's something I do during conflict that helps you feel safe?
- o What's a repair moment that meant a lot to you?
- o What's one thing you wish I understood better about how you handle stress?
- o How do you know when you're ready to reconnect after a disagreement?
- o What's a phrase that helps you feel heard when things get tense?

Reflection Questions

- ♥ When was the last time I discovered something new about my partner?
- ♥ What did I learn about my partner that surprised me?
- ♥ Do I tend to ask questions out of curiosity or out of control?
- ♥ Did I listen with curiosity or with the urge to respond?
- ♥ How did it feel to be heard, or to hear them deeply?
- ♥ What fears hold me back from being more curious?
- ♥ What can I do this week to show that I remembered what they shared?
- ♥ How could curiosity help refresh our relationship right now?

> " To ask is to honour the mystery of your partner

Closing Thought

Curious words are not a form of interrogation or a control technique; they are a profound expression of wonder and discovery. They are your daily commitment to the exhilarating truth that your partner is not a book you've already read to the end, but a still unfolding story, with unexpected twists and new chapters to come.

When you intentionally speak the language of discovery, you refuse to let your partner become a fixture in your life that simply needs managing. You actively ensure they remain a mystery to be explored. This prevents stagnation, keeps the energy of the relationship fresh and is the ultimate safeguard against boredom.

The use of curious words gently reminds both partners that there is always more to know, more to explore and more to share. By asking, listening and seeking to understand, you guarantee that your shared life will not be defined by dull routine, but by continuous, compassionate discovery.

In essence, the language of discovery uses curious words to say, 'I will always want to know you more.'

8. Visionary Words

Why Vision Matters

Visionary Words are the language of hope to whisper, 'Our future matters.'

Every relationship lives in two places at once, first in the immediacy of the present and second in its unfolding story. Couples don't just simply exist together; they are building something with every choice, every habit and every conversation.

In the language of hope, purpose, projection and destiny, visionary words in intentional conversations lift your relationship out of the daily grind and focus your combined energy on what you are actively building together. It's the language that says, 'I see a future with you, and I am excited to build it.'

Couples thrive when they share a sense of direction. When their words not only address today's challenges but also stretch toward tomorrow's possibilities, they infuse their relationship with meaning. Visionary words lift conversations above the daily grind into the realm of dreams and shared purposes. They say, 'This is where we're going. This is what we can build together.'

In the early stages of love, this vision is often implicit – it's the unspoken assumption of 'forever.' But as life accelerates, filled with mortgages, careers, children and complex logistics, couples can forget to keep their long-term vision explicit and current. They become brilliant managers of the present, but accidental architects of the future. They can feel 'busy but disconnected', drifting in reaction to today's demands, without anchoring themselves in a shared tomorrow.

However, with vision, couples find a sense of direction that transforms even the mundane. Preparing dinner becomes part of nourishing a family culture of care. Saving money becomes part of building stability for the future. A simple walk together becomes an investment in long-term health and intimacy. In essence, vision provides not just goals but also a shared narrative of who the couple is becoming.

Research in relational psychology consistently shows that couples who set shared goals report higher satisfaction, deeper intimacy and greater resilience to stress. A shared vision aligns energy, strengthens commitment and creates momentum, especially in difficult times. Whether challenged by financial strain, health issues or family conflict, couples with a vision can frame their struggle as part of a larger journey, not as a dead end.

By speaking a visionary language, you ensure your lives do not just overlap, but are truly interwoven. This practice protects the relationship from being hijacked by circumstance, giving you the shared purpose necessary to weather change and to keep you both excited about your destination. It transforms a stable partnership into one with profound momentum and shared meaning.

Vision does not have to mean such lofty ambitions as building a business or travelling the world (although it can). Sometimes vision is as simple as committing to raising children in a loving environment, prioritising health or nurturing spiritual growth. What matters most is that the vision is shared. It is the sense that 'we are heading somewhere together, and our future is worth investing in.'

What Visionary Words Look Like

The specific, intentional language couples use to define and articulate their shared purpose and future trajectory uses visionary words. Conversations move beyond current tasks to address the partnership's *destination*, transforming a day-to-day routine into a unified, focused journey.

A relationship built only on clear words (managing logistics) and repairing words (solving conflicts) may be stable, but it can also feel stagnant. It functions efficiently, but without emotional momentum. It risks becoming less a passionate life partnership and more a well-run business partnership.

Visionary words bridge that gap. They lift conversations out of the daily grind into the realm of possibility. This language is not merely about planning a holiday or saving for a deposit; it is about *co-creation* – the continuous, intentional act of moving from 'my future' to 'our future.' It asks, discusses and agrees upon the big questions that anchor your shared journey, ensuring that you grow together and not just parallel to one another. It keeps love forward-facing.

Visionary words sound like curiosity infused with hope and direction. They invite both partners to ask, imagine and align around what truly matters, the deeper 'why' behind their journey together. Visionary words honour the fact that a strong present bond is sustained by a shared horizon.

When couples speak this language, they replace drift with direction and routine with renewal. Visionary words turn togetherness into a story with purpose – a future worth walking toward, hand in hand. They remind couples that love isn't just about solving problems, it is also about building something beautiful together.

Visionary words perform four critical functions in a long-term relationship:

1. Inspire – painting the picture of potential
   Visionary words inspire by transforming abstract desires into tangible potential. They paint vivid, compelling pictures of what could be – whether it's the feeling of your future home, the atmosphere you want to cultivate for your children or the quiet joy of a shared retirement goal – this shared narrative is incredibly motivating, as it reminds both partners that current struggles are steps to a beautiful, co-created reality.
2. Unite – creating a shared sense of direction
   This language unites couples by forging a shared sense of direction that transcends individual paths; it clarifies that you are on the same team, moving toward the same horizon. By clearly articulating goals related to finances, careers, values and lifestyle, visionary words eliminate ambiguity and ensure both partners make present choices that honour their mutual commitment to the future.
3. Motivate – enduring difficulties with energy
   Visionary words provide the motivation necessary to endure difficulties; when daily life becomes hard – career paths stall, financial stress hits, a serious setback occurs – the conversation can quickly become exhausting. In these moments, recalling the shared vision acts as a powerful energy source, providing the 'pull' needed to get through the present struggle; reminding the couple that a temporary sacrifice is worthwhile because the collective prize is so compelling.
4. Anchor – remembering the 'why'
   Visionary words anchor the relationship to its

fundamental purpose by crystallising and articulating the couple's underlying 'why', the core set of values that brought and keeps them together. These words serve as a vital reference point, especially during conflict, reminding partners that their bond is stronger than the immediate hurdle and that they are fundamentally committed to their shared life.

From Planning to Co-Creating

When you use visionary words, you elevate the conversation from the transactional to the transformational, given three essential areas of co-creation.

1. Defining Your Future Identity

This is about designing who you want to become, as a unit. It requires stepping outside individual goals and discussing the collective 'we' you are building. It helps eliminate the feeling that your life together is merely happening *to* you.

- What legacy do we want to create? (e.g. legacy of kindness, adventure or learning)
- What does 'success' look like for our family, not just our careers? (defining success in relational terms)
- What kind of person do you hope I grow into, and how can I help you get there?

2. Designing the Emotional Environment

Your home and shared life are not simply physical spaces; they are emotional environments. Visionary words help you design the atmosphere you want to live in.

- What are the three most important feelings we want our home to consistently inspire? (e.g. safety, humour, calm)

- How do we want to feel when we greet each other after a long day?
- What rituals can we commit to that intentionally bring joy and connection into our week?

> Love thrives when couples dream in the same direction

3. Anchoring to a Higher Purpose

This is the highest level of visionary words. They connect your relationship to something larger than yourselves, offering resilience when daily life gets difficult.

- What is the one major goal we want to achieve together in the next five years?
- What is a community or cause we both believe in that we could serve together?
- What's a dream you haven't shared with me yet?

By consistently asking these kinds of questions, you transform your partnership into a powerful force for intentional growth. Visionary words remind you that every small act of communication is building a grand, shared design.

Finding Vision Again

After fifteen years of marriage, Claire and Joseph found themselves stuck in a rut. Most of their conversations revolved around school schedules, bills and who would pick up the groceries. They weren't fighting, but they weren't dreaming either. Claire often thought, 'We're managing life together, but are we really living it?'

One evening, while out on a walk, Joseph asked almost offhandedly, 'Where do you see us in five years?' The question caught Claire by surprise. She hesitated at first, but then said, 'I'd love us to have more time for travel, even just local trips. And I'd like to feel we're building something beyond just paying bills.'

A new door was flung open by that conversation. Over the following weeks, they began talking more intentionally about what they wanted for their family, their health and even their relationship. They set small goals: saving for a weekend away; committing to a regular date night; planning to volunteer together at their community centre.

Claire later reflected, 'It wasn't about the trips or the projects. It was about knowing we were moving together. That gave me hope again.'

Their life didn't suddenly become easy – work stress and parenting demands were still there – but vision reframed their daily routines. Chores became teamwork. Saving became a shared mission. Conversations shifted from 'What do we ***have*** to do today?' to 'What are we building for tomorrow?'

Absence of Vision

Without visionary words, couples may survive but rarely thrive. They risk becoming:

- Reactive – always responding to problems, never shaping the future
- Stagnant – losing energy and excitement
- Disconnected – each partner moving in a different direction.

I once heard a couple say, 'We're good roommates, but not really partners anymore.' They lacked a shared vision and it left them drifting.

> Visionary words turn shared dreams into shared direction

Reflection Exercise: Writing Your Shared Vision Statement

The purpose of this exercise is to help couples move beyond daily routine to create a shared direction for their relationship.

1. Dream individually: take 5–10 minutes each to jot down responses to these prompts:
    - What do I hope our life looks like in 5 years?
    - What are three things I want us to experience together?
    - How do I want us to feel in our relationship?
2. Share your dreams: take turns reading your notes aloud.
    - As you listen, try not to debate or critique – simply listen with curiosity and optimism
    - Circle any themes or overlaps you notice
3. Create a shared statement: work together to write 2–3 sentences that capture your shared vision; for example
    - We want our home to be a place of warmth, laughter and welcome.
    - We will prioritise time together, no matter how busy life gets
    - We want to grow in love, faith and generosity as we journey through life side by side
4. Choose one small step: decide on one practical action you can take this week that aligns with your shared vision; for example
    - Planning a date
    - Starting a savings jar
    - Blocking out family time
5. Revisit regularly: post your vision statement somewhere visible – on the fridge, in your journal or even framed on

the wall. Revisit it monthly to check whether your words, choices and habits are moving you closer to this vision.

Remember: A vision statement is not about perfection. It's about direction. Even small steps, taken consistently, can transform the path of your relationship.

> " Vision is the map that turns todays choices into tomorrows legacy

Power of Shared Vision

A shared vision is far more than a romantic ideal; it is a robust, scientifically supported foundation for resilient, long-term relationships. Visionary words create this foundation by giving couples the necessary frame of reference to navigate difficulty and to maximise joy.

Psychological and Relational Benefits

Research in positive psychology consistently demonstrates that couples who actively create and pursue shared goals report a higher relationship satisfaction, increased resilience and a significantly stronger sense of long-term commitment. A powerful sense of common purpose achieves three key relational outcomes:

1. Reframing challenges: when couples share a vision, daily struggles take on new meaning. Financial sacrifices, long work hours or parenting challenges no longer feel like random, frustrating stumbling blocks.

Instead, they are interpreted as intentional investments in a mutually desired future. For instance, saving money might feel restrictive in the moment, but when both partners agree it is part of building stability for a future family home, it becomes purposeful and unifying.

2. Increased alignment: when long-term goals are clearly articulated, short-term decisions become remarkably easier. Couples with vision use their shared future as a filter, 'Does this choice move us closer to what we said we're building?' This alignment dramatically reduces unnecessary friction and frees up emotional energy that would otherwise be spent on conflict, redirecting it toward connection, creativity and joy.
3. Enhanced resilience: navigating a career shift or relocating for one partner's job can be intensely stressful, but couples with a shared vision interpret it not as a personal sacrifice, but as a temporary phase of a longer journey they are committed to taking together. This collective interpretation strengthens their ability to withstand stress.

Neuroscience of Co-Creation

Neuroscience adds a vital layer to this insight. The act of planning and pursuing meaningful, shared goals activates the brain's reward system, triggering the release of bonding chemicals, such as dopamine and oxytocin. This means that visionary words don't just give couples direction; they literally strengthen their emotional 'glue.' Working toward a common future makes the relationship itself feel more rewarding, reinforcing the drive to seek out and repeat joint, goal-oriented behaviour.

Ultimately, vision is much more than setting arbitrary goals;

it is about crafting a powerful shared narrative that defines your joint identity. It answers the fundamental questions: Who are we becoming? Where are we going? What do we want our love to stand for? When couples keep explicit answers in view, they experience profound momentum and growth, ensuring their relationship moves forward with unwavering purpose.

TURN STRESS INTO SHARED PURPOSE

When Daniel and Amara first got married, money quickly became their biggest source of conflict. Daniel wanted to save aggressively for the future, while Amara felt trapped by constant restrictions and longed for more freedom to enjoy the present. Their arguments often ended in a stalemate, leaving both frustrated and misunderstood.

After a number of counselling sessions, everything changed when they sat down one evening to talk not just about money, but about vision. Instead of debating every expense, they asked each other, 'What are we really trying to build together?' Through that conversation, they realised they both wanted the same outcomes: to buy a home in which to raise a family; to have the freedom to travel occasionally.

Suddenly, saving didn't feel like Daniel's rigid rule or Amara's sacrifice. It became a shared mission. They started calling their savings account their 'home-and-adventure fund', and each contribution became a small step toward their dreams. Amara later said, 'It stopped feeling like he was against me. We were finally pulling in the same direction.'

The financial strain didn't disappear overnight, but their fights reduced dramatically. Instead of draining energy on conflict, they channelled it into teamwork. Daniel and Amara's shared vision turned division into cohesion, which gave their relationship new momentum.

> Without vision, love drifts; with vision, it sails

Barriers to Vision: Why the Future Gets Lost

If visionary words are so powerful, why do couples allow their conversations about the future to fade? The answer lies in the subtle but relentless pressure of daily life and in the internal fears that make bold planning feel risky. These barriers prevent partnerships from achieving their full potential.

1. Focus Obstacles: Tyranny of the Immediate

These barriers arise when couples become overwhelmed by the logistics of the present, allowing the urgent to continually override the important.

- Short-term focus: the primary killer of vision. Couples become so skilled at managing immediate crises (bills, school runs, house repairs) that they lose the habit of looking up. They become excellent co-managers of a routine, but the relationship stagnates because they stop talking about goals that lie beyond the next fortnight
- Exhaustion (survival mode): when partners are too tired, financially strained or mentally drained, their focus shrinks to mere survival. Visionary conversations require emotional energy and optimism, which are unavailable when you are running on empty. You can't plan a future if you're simply trying to get through the day
- Conflicting priorities: partners may have a vision, but their individual dreams have diverged; one may be prioritising career advancement, the other financial stability or relocation. Without a visionary language to bridge these separate desires and find a unifying 'third

way', unaddressed conflicts become a persistent drag on the relationship's momentum.

2. Emotional Obstacles: Fear of Dreaming

These internal, protective mechanisms discourage couples from putting their hopes into words.

- ♥ Fear of disappointment: putting a shared dream into words – a move abroad, a career change, a desired family structure – makes it real and, therefore, makes its failure feel real too. Couples may subconsciously avoid bold conversations to protect themselves from the pain of a dream that might not come true. They choose the safety of the present over the risk of future disappointment
- ♥ Anxiety about lack of agreement: visionary conversations can expose where the couple is not yet aligned. The fear of discovering that they want fundamentally different things can cause partners to avoid the topic altogether, which means they forfeit the chance to work through their differences to chart a mutually exciting course.

Learning to overcome these barriers means intentionally scheduling time and creating the emotional safety required to elevate the conversation beyond the immediate, allowing your relationship to harness its full power.

> " Dreaming together is one of loves deepest acts of trust

Building a Legacy

One couple I worked with, Ade and Ola, realised they had never spoken about their long-term dreams. When they finally did, Ade shared his hope of starting a family business, while Ola dreamed of mentoring younger couples. They decided to blend their visions, creating a family enterprise that included mentoring others. Years later, they reflected, 'That conversation changed our lives. It gave us a mission.'

Can you imagine a newspaper headline about your relationship five years from now? Write it down: 'Couple launches community project together' or 'Partners celebrate decade of shared adventures.' Whatever you imagine, let it spark a conversation of hope.

> Love thrives when couples dream in the same direction

Practical Exercises

Ways to Practise Visionary Words

- ♥ Dream together – regularly ask, 'what do we want for our future?'
- ♥ Set vision nights – dedicate time to dreaming together
- ♥ Make a vision board – use images, words or drawings to picture your goals
- ♥ Link dreams to action – turn visions into practical steps
- ♥ Set shared goals – agree on practical steps toward your vision

- ♥ Celebrate progress – acknowledge milestones, however small
- ♥ Create rituals of vision – annual vision nights, shared journals or goal-setting retreats
- ♥ Keep it alive – revisit and refresh your vision regularly
- ♥ Blend individual and shared dreams – honour both uniqueness and togetherness
- ♥ Speak hope in hard times – remind each other, 'this is temporary. We're building something bigger.'

Vision Night

Set aside an evening and, together, answer these questions:

- ♥ Where do we want to be in 1 year?
- ♥ In 5 years?
- ♥ In 10 years?
- ♥ What values do we want to guide our relationship?
- ♥ What dreams do we want to pursue individually and together?

Write your answers in a shared journal. Review them every few months, updating them as life evolves.

Reflection Questions

- ♥ What shared dreams excite us most right now?
- ♥ When was the last time we spoke about our five- or ten-year vision?
- ♥ How do our daily routines align (or not) with our bigger goals?
- ♥ What words of hope or vision could I speak to my partner this week?

Closing Thought

Visionary words give momentum to a resilient relationship. They function as an emotional anchor set firmly in the future, providing the necessary 'pull' to transform ordinary routines into purposeful, meaningful progress.

These conversations are essential because they consistently remind couples not only of where they are today but also, crucially, of the extraordinary destination they committed to together. This shared perspective creates emotional energy, aligns short-term decisions and builds unwavering resilience.

Couples who neglect this language doom their relationship to drift, passively carried by life's currents. Whereas couples who intentionally speak the language of vision actively set their own course, thriving through a collective sense of purpose.

In essence, the language of hope uses visionary words to say, 'Our best days are still ahead of us.'

Part III.
Practice

9. Putting The Six Languages Together

From Pieces to a Whole

Each of the six emotionally intelligent languages you've explored carries powerful words of its own:

1. Affirming words – the language of recognition
2. Empathic words – the language of presence
3. Clear words – the language of safety
4. Repairing words – the language of healing
5. Curious words – the language of discovery
6. Visionary words – the language of hope.

A single affirming word can brighten a day; an empathic word can soften conflict; a clear word can prevent misunderstanding; a repairing word can save a relationship from bitterness; a curious word can open new doors; and a visionary word can renew hope. Yet, their true strength is revealed only when they are woven together in the rhythm of communication.

Think of them as music: a single instrument can sound a melody, but an orchestra creates a full-blown harmony. In the same way, the six languages work as a kind of symphony, best when practised together. Each plays its part, and together they create an atmosphere which not only maintains love but also deepens it.

When couples rely on only one or two languages,

their relationship may feel lopsided. For instance, constant affirmation without clarity can leave important issues unspoken. Repair without vision may heal wounds but fails to inspire growth. Curiosity without empathy can turn connection into interrogation. But when all six languages are integrated, they balance and strengthen each other.

Affirming words nurture worth; empathic words provide safety; clear words ensure honesty; repairing words restore trust; curious words keep love alive and dynamic; visionary words give direction. Together, they form a holistic way of speaking and being that sustains a relationship through both everyday moments and life's greatest challenges.

The goal is not perfection but integration. You don't need to speak each language flawlessly; you simply need to practise weaving them into the fabric of your daily life. Over time, couples who learn to move fluidly between these six languages discover that their communication becomes richer, their conflicts less threatening and their love more resilient.

Ultimately, these languages are not techniques to be mastered but habits to be deepened. They are a way of relating that says: 'I see you. I hear you. I am safe with you. I am willing to grow with you. I want to discover more of you. And I believe in the future we are building together.'

That is the power of turning pieces into a whole, transforming six separate languages into one emotionally intelligent way of speaking love.

> " The languages are powerful alone
> but transformative together

Why Integration Matters

Couples sometimes make the mistake of approaching these six languages as a checklist: master one, then move on to the next. They might be exceptional at affirming words but habitually avoid repairing words. Or they might prioritise clear words in a disagreement but struggle to introduce empathic words.

The truth is, a thriving relationship is dynamic, not static. Different emotional moments call for different words, and the ability to shift fluently between languages is the ultimate marker of relational health.

Think of these six languages as the musical score to your relationship. You wouldn't play it using only one note or one instrument; its power is in the harmony and dynamic range.

Table 9.1 Language integration

Relational Moment	**Language Needed**	**Outcome**
Moments of joy	Affirming words	Keeps the connection feeling alive and valued
Moments of pain	Empathic words	Makes the emotional load bearable and shared
Times of confusion	Clear words	Restores mutual understanding and focus
After conflict	Repairing words	Rebuilds trust and ensures the bond is mended
To avoid stagnation	Curious words	Reopens doors to discovery and passion
To stay aligned	Visionary words	Provides momentum and pulls you forward together

Integration means developing true relational fluency, being able to move through this entire spectrum as the situation demands. It means you stop defaulting to the one language you're comfortable with and start consciously choosing the one that will best serve the moment. This integrated approach is what transforms a stable partnership into one capable of dynamic resilience.

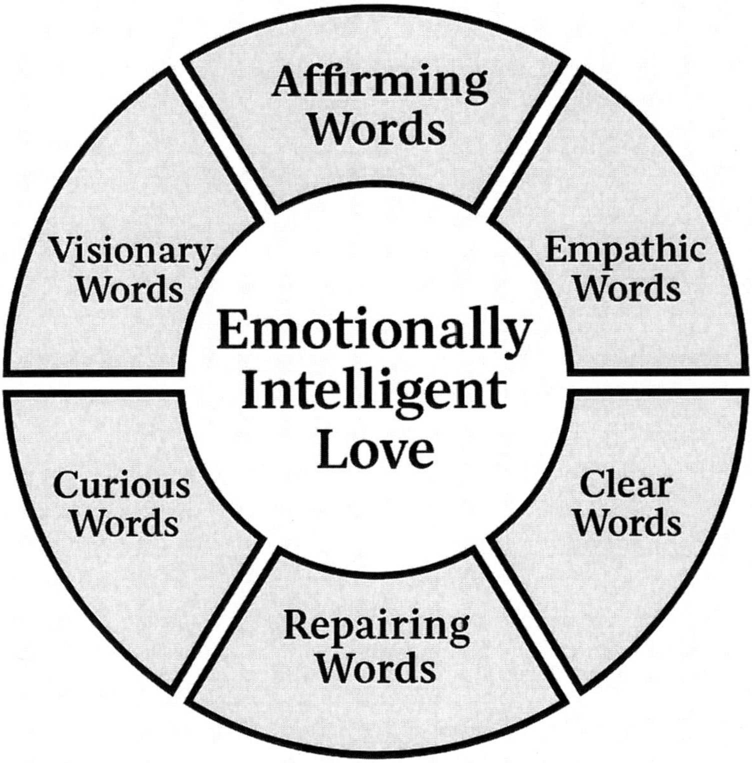

Figure 9.1 Emotionally intelligent love

> Healthy communication is a rhythm, not a one-time act

Relational Compass

When life gets messy, couples can find themselves asking: 'Where do we go from here?' Arguments, disappointments or misunderstandings can leave both partners feeling lost, unsure how to move forward. The Relational Compass is a simple, memorable guide for navigating these moments. Just as a compass helps travellers orient themselves in unfamiliar terrain, this tool helps couples orient their hearts toward the words they need most at any given moment.

- ♥ Centre = empathic and clear words
  Grounding forces that keep the compass steady; empathic words ensure presence for the emotional safety of feeling understood; clear words provide truth for the intellectual safety of being honest and direct. Together, they anchor every other direction, ensuring the compass doesn't spin out of control
- ♥ North = affirming words
  The upward movement of recognition and encouragement. When a relationship feels weighed down by criticism or neglect, turning north reminds couples to speak words of truth that lift, affirm and recognise one another's worth
- ♥ South = repairing words
  The downward move into humility, apology and restoration. When trust has been broken or tempers have flared, south is the path of lowering pride, taking responsibility and seeking to restore what has been hurt
- ♥ East = curious words
  The sunrise of new beginnings, questions and discovery. When boredom sets in or assumptions harden, east invites couples to look with fresh eyes, to explore each

other's evolving inner world and to awaken the spirit of discovery

- West = visionary words
  The sunset horizon represents direction, legacy and shared dreams. When life feels aimless or routines consume energy, west reminds couples to lift their gaze and speak about where they are heading together, what they want to build and who they are becoming.

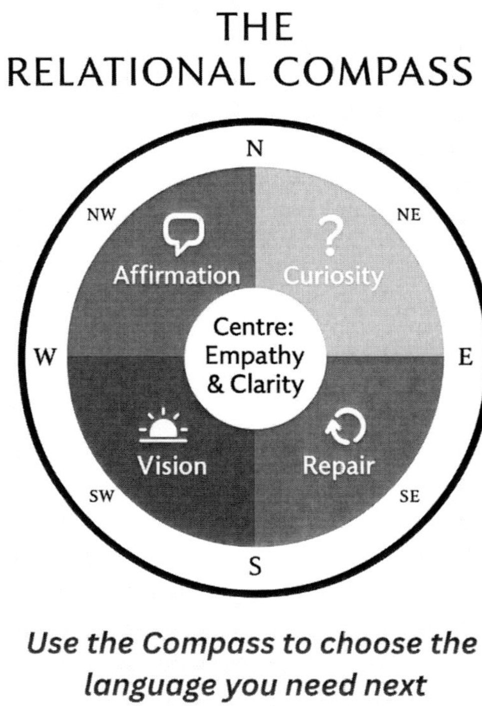

Figure 9.2 Relational compass

As for many of the concepts in this book, the Relational Compass is not about perfection, but about orientation.

When couples feel lost in conflict, they can pause and ask: 'Which direction do we need most right now?' Sometimes it's affirmation, sometimes repair, sometimes vision. At other times, it's simply returning to the centre, grounding themselves in empathy and clarity before moving forward.

Similar to any compass, it doesn't remove the challenges of the journey, but it does ensure couples don't wander without direction. It offers hope that, even in confusion, there is always a way back to connection.

> Integration turns scattered skills into a lifestyle of love

Using the Relational Compass in Real Time

When conflict arises, couples can use the Relational Compass as a quick guide to regain direction and connection.

1. Pause the spiral
    - When you notice the argument is escalating or going in circles, take a breath and call a pause. One partner can ask: 'Which direction do we need right now?'
2. Choose a direction together
    - Centre (empathic and clear words): do we need to ground ourselves in presence and honesty first?
    - North (affirming words): do we need encouragement or recognition?
    - South (repairing words): do we need humility, apology or forgiveness?
    - East (curious words): do we need to ask open questions and explore, rather than assume?

   - West (visionary words): do we need to step back and remember our bigger picture or shared goals?

3. Take a small action
   - If it's repair, offer a sincere apology
   - If it's empathy, reflect your partner's feelings back to them
   - If it's vision, lift the conversation toward hope or direction.

4. Reconnect before resolving
   - Don't rush to solve the issue immediately. Focus first on re-establishing safety and connection.
   - Once you're both steady, you can return to problem-solving with a calmer mindset.

FINDING A BEARING

James and Pam had been married for eight years, during which they had learned each other's strengths and weaknesses. But, like many couples, they sometimes found themselves caught up in arguments that spiralled out of control. One evening, what started as a small disagreement over household chores quickly escalated. Voices rose, defences went up, and soon both felt stuck in a familiar stalemate – frustrated, unheard and misunderstood.

In the past, they would have withdrawn into silence, sometimes for hours or even days, letting the tension linger. But this time was different. Pam remembered the Relational Compass they had recently discussed. Taking a breath, she said gently, 'Wait – which direction do we need right now?'

Her question shifted the atmosphere. Instead of pushing his point harder, James paused to reflect. After a moment he replied, 'South. I need to repair.' His words softened the air between them. Looking directly at her, he added, 'I'm sorry for snapping. I let my stress get the better of me and I know I hurt you.'

Pam felt her defensiveness melt. She didn't need him to be perfect; she needed him to take responsibility. She responded with empathy, saying, 'I know it's been a hard week for you. Thank you for saying that.'

What could have been another night of distance became a moment of reconnection. By turning to the Relational Compass, James and Pam found the words they needed most in that moment so they could move out of the spiral and back to safety.

Pam later reflected, 'We didn't solve everything in that conversation, but we stopped the bleeding. We reminded ourselves that the relationship matters more than the argument.'

The Relational Compass didn't erase their conflict, but it gave them a bearing. And sometimes, knowing which direction to turn to is enough to find your way home.

Remember: The Relational Compass doesn't fix your conflict, it helps you find the right starting point for moving forward together

---

> Connection deepens when all six languages are spoken in harmony

Why the Relational Compass Works

- It's visual – you can picture it quickly in your mind
- It's flexible – works in moments of conflict, joy or planning
- It's grounding – helps you slow down and choose intentional language instead of reacting
- It's balanced – reminds us that all six languages matter, not just our favourites.

Finding Balance

Adele and Jonas were excellent at empathy and affirmation, but they avoided repair and clarity. Small tensions kept building into big blow-ups. Once they began using the Relational Compass and weekly check-ins, they discovered their imbalance. Jonas later reflected, 'We realised we were strong in warmth but weak in honesty. The compass pushed us to practise the languages we'd neglected.'

> Integration is not perfection, but practice made consistent

Practical Exercises

Compass Check

Draw the Relational Compass together on a piece of paper and place it somewhere visible at home (like the fridge or the bedroom wall). For one week, practice pausing during tense or important conversations to ask: which direction does our relationship need right now?

At the end of the week, discuss what patterns emerged; and whether using the compass helped you reset more quickly.

Daily Integration

Beyond the compass, integration means weaving multiple languages into everyday life. For example:

- ♥ Begin the day with affirming words

- Use clear words during logistical conversations
- Practise curious words over dinner
- Offer repairing words if tensions arise
- Close the evening with visionary words about the future
- Keep empathic words present throughout.

Integration is less about grand moments and more about consistent small ones.

Weekly Check-In

A practical way to ensure integration is to build a weekly rhythm (see Chapter 11 for more). Go through the six languages as a guide to your check-in:

- Affirming words, 'This week I appreciated ...'
- Empathic words, 'Something that felt heavy for me was ...'
- Clear words, 'Something I'd like to discuss is ...'
- Repairing words, 'I'd like to apologise for ...'
- Curious words, 'A question I'd like to ask you is ...'
- Visionary words, 'Looking ahead, I'd love us to ...'

Reflection Questions

- When we argue, which compass direction do we tend to avoid?
- Which 'point' comes most naturally to me, and which feels hardest?
- How could we make it a habit to pause and ask, 'Where do we need to go right now?'

Closing Thought

The six emotionally intelligent languages are not separate techniques to memorise but a living framework to practise. They are designed to flow together, shaping the climate and direction of a relationship. The Relational Compass is one way to keep them alive and accessible. It reminds couples that in every situation, whether joyful or difficult, there is always a way forward.

In essence, the Relational Compass directs you to a language that says, 'Wherever we are, we can find our way back to each other.'

10. Obstacles and Breakthroughs

Why This Chapter Matters

It's one thing to learn the theory of the six emotionally intelligent languages. It's another to put them into practice in the heat of real life – as tempers flare, given deeply ingrained habits and under overwhelming stress. Every couple, no matter how strong or committed, encounters resistance. The question is not *if* obstacles will come, but *how* we respond when they do.

Obstacles can feel like walls in the form of:

- Communication breakdowns when conversations go round in circles or end in silence
- Cycles of conflict in which the same arguments keep resurfacing
- Financial stress that weighs heavily on decision-making and security
- Family pressure from relatives, parenting struggles or differing cultural expectations
- Health challenges that disrupt routines and test patience
- Simply the fatigue of everyday life, when the demands of work, chores and responsibilities drain the energy needed for connection.

At times, these walls seem solid and immovable. Couples feel trapped, seeing themselves on opposite sides, with no way through. Yet walls can become doors if approached with the right tools – and those tools are found in the six emotionally intelligent languages.

Breakthroughs emerge not because obstacles disappear, but because couples learn to face them together. When a partner says, 'I see how this is affecting you' (empathic words), or 'I'm sorry I added to the stress' (repairing words), walls begin to crack. When they ask, 'how can we navigate this as a team?' (curious words), or remind each other, 'this challenge won't define us; we have a bigger vision' (visionary words), a doorway suddenly appears.

Use of the six emotionally intelligent languages doesn't remove hardship, but it does change how you view, express and navigate it. Instead of feeling like adversaries, couples discover they can stand side by side, to address the obstacle together. Over time, these moments of breakthrough build resilience and trust, showing both partners that their love is not fragile, that it can endure and adapt, and even grow stronger under pressure.

Obstacles, then, are not only tests of love but are also opportunities for love to cut through the walls of conflict and resentment to a place where the practice of the six languages in real time turns theory into lived reality. And each breakthrough becomes part of the couple's story, evidence that love is not defeated by difficulty but reignited by it.

> " Conflict doesnt define couples,
> how they recover does

Common Obstacles Couples Face

Adopting a new vocabulary of connection isn't always smooth. As couples strive for fluency in the six emotionally intelligent languages, they inevitably confront deeply ingrained behavioural patterns and emotional hurdles. There are five common obstacles to integrating the full framework.

1. Inherited Scripts

Many of us grew up in families where essential relational languages were absent or poorly modelled. If affirming or repairing words were rarely used, practising them as an adult feels awkward, unnatural or forced as old patterns impose themselves. Lack of a positive emotional script means couples have to actively *re-learn* basic communication.

For example, one partner may find it nearly impossible to apologise genuinely because they never witnessed a sincere apology being offered or accepted in their childhood home.

2. Emotional Triggers and Hypersensitivity

Old, unhealed wounds often surface in intimate relationships. Past hurts can leave us hypersensitive to tone and intent. Words that sound neutral or factual to one partner may feel loaded, critical or triggering to the other.

For instance, a simple request for clear words about a joint decision may be heard by a partner with an underlying wound as a direct and painful criticism of their competence, which shuts down the conversation before it even starts.

3. Misaligned Paces

Partners rarely move at the same speed. One partner may embrace all six languages enthusiastically, viewing them as a useful toolkit, while the other resists because they find them overwhelming or unnecessary. This mismatch in effort and pace often causes intense frustration.

A sincere attempt by one partner to use repairing words and move on from a past hurt may be met with reluctance or suspicion by the other, leaving the initiator feeling exposed and rejected.

4. Defaulting to Survival Mode

Under periods of intense pressure, stress or fatigue, couples nearly always default to a survival mode of communication. In these moments, clear words are quickly replaced by snapping, and empathic words vanish. Instead of using objective language to describe the problem, couples resort to exhausting, reactive, subjective outbursts. Higher-level languages are the first casualties, leaving the partnership vulnerable to needless conflict.

5. Fear of Vulnerability

Speaking an emotionally intelligent language offers a degree of risk. Affirming words could be rejected if the compliment isn't received. Repairing words mean having to swallow one's pride. Visionary words risk future disappointment if the goal isn't met. When trust has previously been broken, this necessary vulnerability can feel profoundly unsafe, leading to avoidance. The fear of being honest or exposed causes partners to retreat, allowing silence to descend into complete emotional withdrawal.

> Breakthroughs often hide inside the very barriers we resist

Breakthrough Principles

1. Progress Over Perfection

One of the biggest barriers is the belief that we must 'get it right' every time. Couples may feel discouraged when they fall back into old habits. But the goal is not perfection; it is progress.

- Each attempt at empathy, even if clumsy, matters
- Each repair attempt, even if imperfect, counts
- Each affirmation, even if small, builds momentum.

The key is to notice growth rather than failure.

Health Challenges

Elena's chronic illness often left her exhausted, and her partner Sam sometimes felt resentful about carrying more of the load. One night, instead of withdrawing, Sam used curious words to ask gently, 'What's the hardest part of this for you?'

Elena, with tears in her eyes, shared how guilty she felt for slowing them down. Sam responded using visionary and affirming words, 'I don't want you to carry that guilt. We'll figure this out together.' In that moment, the illness was no longer a wedge between them – it became something they faced side by side.

2. Slow the Moment

Obstacles often arise because we react too quickly. We speak before thinking, defend before listening or withdraw before clarifying. A breakthrough comes when we slow the moment.

- ♥ Take a breath before replying
- ♥ Ask yourself, 'Which language does this moment need?'
- ♥ Respond with intention, not instinct.

Even a pause of a few seconds can shift the whole climate.

Financial Strain

When Leah and Marcus faced an unexpected job loss, money quickly became a source of tension. Arguments flared over budgeting, each accusing the other of being careless or controlling. One evening, Marcus paused mid-argument and used repairing and empathic words to say, 'I know you're scared. I am too. I shouldn't have blamed you.'

Leah softened and replied, 'Thank you for saying that. It's reassuring to know we're on the same team.'

That moment didn't solve their financial situation, but it broke the cycle of blame. They began working together on a plan, shifting from being adversaries to becoming allies.

3. Practise in Safe Spaces

It's hard to practise new skills in the middle of heated conflict. Couples find breakthroughs when they practise in calmer, everyday moments:

- ♥ Affirmation can begin with a small thank-you
- ♥ Empathy can start with listening to a minor frustration
- ♥ Vision can begin with a light-hearted question about the weekend.

The more these languages are practised in safety, the more available they become in moments of relational stress.

Frustration to Breakthrough

Elaine and Rob struggled with clarity. Rob tended to be vague, while Elaine grew frustrated and demanded more detail. Their conversations spiralled as a result.

Their breakthrough came when they agreed to practise 'clarity check-ins' once a week, outside of conflict. Rob learned to be more specific, Elaine learned to ask gently for clarification. Over time, their heated arguments diminished.

Elaine reflected, 'The breakthrough wasn't instant. It came slowly, as we created new habits.'

4. Celebrate Small Wins

Couples can overlook progress because they focus on what's still missing. This is unfortunate because breakthroughs come when we pause intentionally to celebrate small victories.

- 'We apologised quicker this time'
- 'We asked more questions this week'
- 'We spoke about our future, even briefly.'

Celebration reinforces progress and motivates continued growth. Hanging on failures blinds progress and stifles growth.

Recurring Conflict

Faith and Lola kept arguing about housework, each feeling unseen. One Saturday morning, after yet another tense exchange, Lola took a breath and found affirming plus repairing words to say, 'I love you, and I don't want this to keep getting between us.'

Faith, caught off guard, lowered his tone and replied, 'Okay, let's be clear about what we both need.'

Together, they worked out a plan and while chores didn't disappear resentment did. The language of clarity and repair turned a stuck cycle into a manageable system.

> Obstacles are invitations to grow together

Practical Exercises

Obstacle Map

1. Write down the biggest communication obstacles you face as a couple (e.g. defensiveness, avoiding repair, lack of time)
2. Next to each, write which language could best help overcome it, such as:

Obstacle	**Language**
Avoiding apology	Repair words
Feeling unseen	Affirming words

3. Choose one obstacle and one language to focus on during the following week
4. At the end of the week, reflect together on what changed and what still requires reviewing
5. Commit to continuing the process until you are both satisfied with the results.

Forgiveness Breakthrough

Darius and Emma carried resentments for years. Arguments ended without repair. Both felt stuck. Their breakthrough came when they practised the 'Anatomy of a Good Apology' (see Chapter 6).

For the first time, Darius admitted, 'I was wrong, and I see how it hurt you.' Emma wept, not from pain but from relief.

Emma later said, 'That moment was a long-awaited doorway. It didn't fix everything instantly, but it gave us hope again.'

Breakthrough Habits: Fostering Relational Progress

True communication breakthroughs rarely happen by accident; they are the result of adopting and consistently practising deliberate habits. To move past old patterns and make the six emotionally intelligent languages your default response, integrate the following three practices into your daily life.

1. Shift Your Mindset

Breakthroughs begin with an internal choice to interrupt reactive patterns.

- Pause before reacting: when you feel an emotional trigger, an urge to defend or a need to snap back, institute a physical pause. Take a deliberate breath and create a moment of vital space between the stimulus and your response. This brief pause is your chance to choose an intentional language over a default reaction
- Name the language: use your framework as an active diagnostic tool. When faced with tension or confusion, consciously ask yourself which language this situation requires. Is it empathic words to validate the pain, or clear words to define the problem? This simple question instantly shifts the interaction from conflict to collaboration.

2. Sustain the Effort

Breakthroughs are maintained through patience and external support.

- Celebrate small wins: the most significant transformation often comes gradually, not dramatically. Actively acknowledge and celebrate small improvements – a successful use of repairing words; a moment of unexpected curiosity; or a difficult boundary set with clear words. Celebrating progress reinforces the new habits and motivates you to keep going.
- Seek external support: some relational patterns are too entrenched to be resolved solely by those involved. Recognise when a breakthrough requires an outside perspective. Don't hesitate to seek the objective guidance of a counsellor, a mentor or a trusted third party. Viewing support as a strength, not a failure, is a sign of true relational maturity.

3. Commit to Repetition

- Do it all over again: ultimately, new and enabling habits are built through repetitive action. A single successful use of a new language is just the beginning. Commit to the process of intentional communication every day. It is consistency, even when imperfect, that hardwires breakthrough languages into the automatic rhythms of your relationship.

> " Resilience is built in the messy middle, not just the happy ending

Reflection Questions

- Which of the six languages feels hardest for us to practise consistently? Why?
- What old patterns from our past make certain languages feel unfamiliar?
- How do we usually respond when stress overwhelms us
- How could we reset more gently?
- What small wins have we already experienced as we've tried to practise these languages?

Closing Thought

Obstacles are inevitable, they are not a sign of failure, they are invitations to grow. Every couple will stumble as they learn to speak the six languages. But each obstacle contains within it the seed of a breakthrough. Couples who practise the six emotionally intelligent languages consistently discover that every challenge holds the potential for deeper intimacy.

In essence, obstacles become breakthroughs when couples choose words that heal, connect and inspire hope.

> Every breakdown holds the seed of a breakthrough

11. Practical Tools and Daily Rhythms

Why Rhythms Matter

Overcoming the Knowledge–Action Gap

Knowledge of the six emotionally intelligent languages is a powerful first step, but knowledge alone isn't enough. Many couples find themselves caught in what I call the 'knowledge–action gap': they agree with the principles on the page, only for all good intentions to dissolve instantly the moment stress, fatigue or a sudden argument take over. Time and again, I have observed that when the pressure is on, we default to our ingrained habits, which are often the very patterns we're trying to escape.

The key to true, lasting transformation is rhythm – making small, repeatable actions that function like muscle memory for your relationship.

Building Relational Muscle Memory

Just as a healthy body is not built by a single, heroic workout but by the daily, consistent habits of eating well and regular movement, a healthy relationship isn't sustained by occasional grand gestures. It is sustained by consistent, intentional words. The goal isn't to speak perfectly; it's to embed the six languages in the ordinary fabric of life until they become second nature.

Daily rhythms matter because they train the relationship to default toward connection instead of disconnection. Think of them as automated systems in a resilient house:

- ♥ A quick affirming word before leaving the house acts as emotional insulation
- ♥ An empathic word check-in after work functions as a safety valve to stress
- ♥ A brief, honest repairing word after a snappish retort prevents rust.

These rhythms weave a reliable safety net, ensuring that when the inevitable bigger challenges arise, your relationship already has a strong, foundation of practised connection.

> " Love grows in the ordinary, not just the extraordinary

Sustainability in the Chaos of Modern Life

Rhythms also sustain emotionally intelligent languages. In the chaos of juggling jobs, children, deadlines and distractions couples rarely have the time or energy for dramatic, two-hour interventions. What they *can* manage are these daily micro-habits: intentionally pausing to affirm; practising curiosity at the dinner table; repairing quickly; or jointly checking their emotional 'climate' before bed.

These small, manageable acts weave the languages into the everyday, ensuring that love is not only expressed in the big moments, but deeply lived in the ordinary ones. Ultimately, rhythms transform a noble intention – 'We should communicate better' – into a lived identity: 'We are the kind of people who naturally affirm, empathise, clarify, repair, stay curious and envision together.' And when that shift happens, emotionally intelligent languages are no longer just a tool, they become an unconscious, resilient way of life.

Practical Rhythms for the Six Languages

1. Daily Connection Check-In (15-Minute Rule)

This is the most critical rhythm a couple can establish. It formalises the daily act of 'turning toward' your partner, preventing the silent buildup of stress and detachment. Its power lies in its predictability and its brevity as a sacred time dedicated to focused, emotional connection. Implement the check-in by:

1. Scheduling the sanctuary: agree on a 10–15-minute, distraction-free window every day. This is non-negotiable time; it must be protected from phones, children and outside demands. This window is typically right after work or before bed
2. Sharing your day: both partners share their answers to these two simple questions that encourage a balanced look at the day –
    - What was the best part of your day? (Focuses on affirming words and a positive perspective)
    - What was the most challenging part of your day? (Opens the door for empathic words and support)

3. Stress buster rule: when discussing challenges, the listening partner must listen and validate, not solve. Check-in is a time to share the emotional load, not to enter problem-solving mode. Use empathic words to mirror their feelings: 'That sounds incredibly frustrating, love (or whatever your pet name is). I can see why you'd be upset about that.'
4. End with gratitude: always conclude the check-in with a sincere and specific expression of appreciation for your partner or something they did. This reinforces the positive emotional bond (e.g. 'I really appreciate you handling the delivery today; it took a huge thing off my mind.')

2. 'I Feel ... When You ... Because ...' Statement

This tool is the ultimate practice for using clear words and transforming accusations into clear, non-blaming expressions of need. It provides a structured template for a 'soft start-up' to initiate difficult conversations and to assert needs without criticism in a way that minimises defensiveness.

Four-Part Clarity Formula

Table 11.1 Four-part clarity formula

	Focus	Function and Purpose	Example in Practice
I feel ...	Emotion	State a clear, non-judgemental feeling. Crucially, avoid 'I feel like,' which usually hides a thought or judgement	'I feel worried ...'
When you ...	Fact/behaviour	State the specific, observable action or situation (the facts, not your interpretation)	'... when you don't call to say you'll be late ...'

	Focus	Function and Purpose	Example in Practice
Because ...	Impact/ need	Explain the underlying reason, need or emotional impact this behaviour has on you. This promotes empathy in your partner.	'Because I immediately start picturing scenarios where you might be hurt, and I feel vulnerable'
What I need is ...	Request	Make a clear, positive request for future behaviour. This turns a complaint into a solution.	'What I need is a quick text, even if it's just one word, when your schedule changes'

By starting with the impact on yourself rather than the deficiency of your partner, this statement shifts the focus from blame to clarity and co-operation. It opens the door for your partner to hear your need without their defence mechanisms immediately activating.

This works because it shifts the focus from 'You are wrong' to 'This is how your action impacts me', making it easier for your partner to hear and respond constructively.

3. Positive Intent Assumption or 'Listen Like You're Wrong' Mindset

This tool is a mindset shift essential for fostering curiosity and empathy, particularly when you feel criticised or misunderstood. When an issue is raised, your immediate default should not be to defend your intentions, but to seek your partner's truth. Practise this by:

1. Assume positive intent: when your partner brings up a complaint or hurt, consciously remind yourself: 'Their message is not a malicious attack; it is a bid for connection about an unmet need.' This instantly lowers your emotional reactivity.
2. Mindful listening (three steps): instead of jumping to defend or explain, follow this protocol:

- o Paraphrase/Mirror: Repeat back, in your own words, what you heard them say. Start with: 'What I hear you saying is..' This ensures accuracy and makes your partner feel instantly seen.
- o Validate the Feeling: Acknowledge the legitimacy of their emotion, even if you disagree with the facts. Use Empathic Words: 'That makes sense. I can absolutely see why you would feel overlooked in that situation.'
- o Ask Collaborative Questions (Curious Words): If you still feel confused or want to explore the topic deeper, use open-ended questions that invite them to share more. For instance, 'What does feeling truly supported look like for you in this particular context?' or 'Tell me more about the moment that felt the most frustrating.'

This practice transforms potential conflict into a moment of discovery, allowing you to use curious words to understand the deeper story behind the complaint.

> " Daily words, spoken with care, create lasting intimacy

Words to enhance your daily rhythm

1. Affirming words in the language of recognition
   - o Morning boost: begin each day with one affirming statement: 'I'm grateful for how hard you work for us'
   - o Sticky note love: leave a short encouraging note where your partner will find it – on the fridge, the mirror or their laptop
2. Empathic words in the language of presence

   - Daily check-in: ask at least once, 'How are you feeling right now?' then listen without rushing to fix it
   - Reflect back: when your partner shares, mirror their emotions: 'That sounds overwhelming. I can see why you'd feel that way'

3. Clear words in the language of safety
   - Evening clarity moment: spend 5 minutes sharing one clear need for the next day, such as, 'I'll need your help with the school run tomorrow'
   - Ban the guessing game: instead of hinting, practice saying directly what you want such as, 'Could you please ...'

4. Repairing words in the language of healing
   - Quick apologies: if you snap or speak harshly, apologise within the hour rather than letting it linger
   - End-of-day reset: before bed, ask, 'Is there anything I need to apologise for today?'

5. Curious words in the language of discovery
   - One curious question: at dinner or during a walk, ask an open-ended question such as, 'What made you smile today?'
   - Weekly wonder: once a week, ask something bigger such as, 'What's a dream you'd love us to work toward?'

6. Visionary words in the language of hope
   - Shared gratitude: each night, name one thing you're grateful for in your shared life
   - Future talk: once a week, spend 10 minutes dreaming together – even if it's as small as a trip, a project or a way you want to grow as a couple.

These rhythms are not about doing everything at once, but about weaving small, intentional practices into everyday life until they become second nature. Over time, they build a relational culture where emotionally intelligent languages are lived, not just learned.

Weekly Alignment Check-In

Daily practices sustain connection, but weekly rhythms create space for deeper reflection and intentional growth. While daily check-ins keep couples tethered, a weekly check-in allows them to step back, take a breath and look at the bigger picture. This 45–60-minute rhythm is your relationship's maintenance session. It ensures no resentments are left unaddressed (repair) and that your lives are interwoven (clarity and vision). Schedule it for a weekly quiet time, such as a Sunday evening or a calm weekday.

Ground Rules for Safety and Focus

1. Strictly no interruptions: turn off all devices, this time is sacred
2. No new arguments: if a topic gets too heated, agree to pause and schedule a separate 20-minutes for repairing words because this check-in must remain productive
3. Use a timer: dedicate a specific amount of time to each section to ensure you cover everything and don't get stuck on one.

Section 1: Emotional and Relational Climate (15 Minutes)

This section uses empathic and repairing words to clear the air.

1. Repair sweep – each partner takes a turn to ask:
    - 'Is there anything I said or did this past week that created an emotional dent or needs a quick repair?' (This is a low-stakes invitation for accountability)
    - The goal is to quickly address small hurts before they become big resentments. Practise quick, genuine apologies ('I'm sorry for my tone on Tuesday')
2. Affirmation and Appreciation: share at least two specific examples of moments where you felt genuinely connected, loved or supported by your partner this week.
    - The goal is to end this section on a positive note and to practise affirming words.

Section 2: Logistics and Clarity (20 Minutes)

This section ensures you are both using Clear Words to manage your lives effectively.

1. Week ahead – review calendars and logistics:
    - Who is doing what and when for childcare, social plans and so on?
    - Household duties: are chores balanced? Does anything need to be delegated or outsourced?

- 'Big rocks': What are the 1 or 2 major tasks, appointments or deadlines each person needs support with next week?

2. Financial clarity: briefly review the budget, any large upcoming purchases or unexpected expenses.
   - The goal is to prevent surprises and ensure financial decisions align with your vision.

Section 3: Curiosity and Vision (15 Minutes)

This section prevents stagnation by actively engaging with future dreams and personal growth.

1. Curiosity corner: ask an open-ended question that encourages your partner to share a deeper thought or a feeling unrelated to logistics, such as, 'What is one thing you learned about yourself this past week?' or 'What is one small thing we could do to make next week feel easier for you?'
2. Future focus (visionary words): touch base on one medium- or long-term goal, such as, holiday plans, progress on a savings goal or a shared life dream (like a career change or home renovation)
   - The goal is to keep your collective eyes on the visionary horizon.

Action Step: Takeaway

Conclude the check-in by each partner stating one tangible commitment they are making for the relationship or a shared goal in the upcoming week. This ensures the conversation translates into action.

Couples who practise this rhythm often find that small issues never have the chance to snowball into larger problems. Instead of reacting to tension when it erupts, they proactively maintain their connection. Over time, this rhythm becomes a relational 'maintenance check' – a consistent practice that protects intimacy, strengthens trust and keeps love moving in a purposeful direction.

Tip: Choose a regular time and place for your weekly check-in – over Sunday breakfast, during a quiet evening walk or at the end of the week before bed. Consistency matters more than perfection.

30-Minute Sunday Reset

For years, Seye and Lolade felt they were drifting. Their weeks were packed with work, chores and parenting duties, and by Sunday night both were often running on fumes. Arguments flared over small things – who forgot to take out the bins, why bills hadn't been paid – but underneath was a deeper frustration: they felt disconnected.

Then they tried a simple Sunday evening check-in. They set aside just 30 minutes after dinner, phones put away, cups of tea in hand. At first, it felt awkward, but soon it became their favourite ritual of the week.

They used the time to ask each other intentional questions: 'What went well for us this week?' 'What felt heavy?' 'Is there anything I need to apologise for?' 'What are we looking forward to?' These conversations didn't magically erase stress, but they did stop it from piling up unnoticed.

Seye later reflected, 'It's like pressing reset every week. We don't carry issues into Monday anymore.' Lolade agreed, adding, 'I finally feel like we're on the same page before the week begins.'

What once felt like endless tension became an opportunity for connection. The Sunday reset gave them space to clear the air, celebrate small wins and realign their vision. It was only 30 minutes, but it changed the way they carried the other 10,050 minutes of their week.

Monthly Momentum Check-In

The monthly check-in is designed to be a one-hour session dedicated to checking on the momentum of your larger goals and cultivating deeper individual connection. While the weekly session cleans up small issues, the monthly session looks for strategic alignment by integrating curious and visionary words.

Ground Rules for Safety and Focus

- Schedule: block out a specific night each month (e.g. the last Friday or the first Sunday afternoon)
- Change location: hold this meeting outside the house – in a quiet coffee shop, during a walk in the park or on a specific spot on the sofa – to signal that this is different from the daily/weekly routine.

Section 1: Review and Accountability (20 Minutes)

This section ensures that you are tracking progress on your larger commitments.

1. Track the win: revisit the shared goals you established in the annual vision audit. Did you move closer to them this month? Celebrate your progress and identify obstacles
   - The goal is to keep visionary words active and to hold yourselves gently accountable
2. Budget deep dive (clarity): go beyond the weekly glance and use this time for a comprehensive review of spending and savings targets. For instance, ask 'Did our spending this month align with our long-term financial vision, and if not, what needs clarity next month?'
3. Relationship scorecard: score your satisfaction (from 1 to 10) with one specific, targeted area of the relationship (e.g. sex and intimacy, division of chores, quality time). Use clear words to discuss the scores and suggest one practical step for improvement next month.

Section 2: Cultivating Individual Discovery (25 Minutes)

This section uses curious words to ensure you remain connected to your partner's evolving internal life.

1. 'Big three' reflection – each partner shares their answers to three deeper, non-logistical questions:
   - What is something you feel guilty about right now, and what kind of support would you like from me? (invites empathic and repairing words)
   - What has challenged your energy or mental health the most this month? (prompts curious words about their inner world)

- What is one thing you are trying to learn or achieve right now that I might not know about? (focuses on affirmation of their personal growth)

2. Shared fun audit: look at the calendar for the upcoming month. Have you scheduled any dedicated, fun time together? If not, use clear words to book at least one date or activity that fosters joy and connection.

Section 3: Forward Commitment (15 Minutes)

Conclude by looking forward with intention.

1. One small shift (clear words): state one small, concrete action you will personally commit to for the next month to improve one specific area of your communication (e.g. 'I will use the "I feel" statement once a week' or 'I will pause for three seconds before reacting to a criticism')
2. Express confidence: end with a strong statement of affirmation in your partner and the future you are building together.

> Consistency matters more than intensity

Annual Vision Audit (Future-Proofing Your Partnership)

While your daily, weekly and monthly rhythms expertly manage the present and maintain the relationship's momentum, the annual vision audit is dedicated to the panoramic view. Think of it as a captain putting their ship into dry dock once a year for a complete structural inspection and a recalibration of the navigation system.

It's the essential practice of looking up, looking out and ensuring your partnership remains aligned with your biggest, boldest visionary words. This isn't a casual chat; it's a strategic investment in reviewing the entire scope of your shared life to proactively adjust your course for the year ahead.

Schedule one extended session of 3–4 dedicated hours away from the distractions of home, perhaps a quiet weekend afternoon or a special overnight stay. Without this high-level strategy session, even the best daily habits can accidentally steer you toward separate destinations.

Stage 1: Review (Repair and Clarity)

Dedicate the first hour to objectively assessing the last year. Clarity is essential. Focus on facts, not blame or criticism.

1. Relationship health score: rate the relationship from 1 to 10 in the 4 key areas of emotional intimacy, conflict management, shared fun/connection, and physical intimacy. Discuss why you gave the scores you did
2. Unfinished business: surface any lingering hurts or unresolved issues from the past year. Use repairing words to finalise them, ensuring you start the new year with a clean slate
3. Wins and lessons: celebrate the relationship's biggest win from the last year and clearly identify the biggest communication lesson you learned together.

Stage 2: Horizon (Vision and Curiosity)

Dedicate the next two hours to planning and dreaming. This is where your visionary and curious words take centre stage.

1. Personal horizons: each person shares their single most important personal goal or development they intend to pursue in the next year (e.g. a professional course, a new hobby, a health target). The other partner practises curious words and asks: 'How can I support you in that without interfering?'
2. Shared vision check: revisit your biggest life dreams (from your initial visionary words discussions). Are you still aiming for the same kind of home, lifestyle or legacy? Discuss whether any adjustments are needed
3. Next 12 months: define 1–3 shared, measurable visionary goals for the upcoming year (e.g. 'Take one trip without the children', 'Save X amount for the house deposit' or 'Dedicate one evening a week to a shared creative project').

Stage 3: Plan (Clarity and Action)

Conclude by translating the vision into concrete action, using Clear Words.

1. Resource alignment: clearly define what resources (time, money, emotional energy) need to be adjusted to start moving toward the shared goals identified in Stage 2
2. Schedule check-in: set the date for the next annual vision audit to ensure the rhythm is maintained
3. Affirmation: end with a strong verbal affirmation of commitment and excitement for the shared future you've just planned.

These rhythm structures – daily for micro-connection, weekly for maintenance, monthly/annual for strategic growth – provide you with a complete system to elevate your communication above the daily grind and to proactively co-create your destiny. They integrate the six languages in a powerful practice that increases engagement and strengthens connection.

Practical Daily Rhythms for The Six Languages

1. **Affirming Words** - the Language of Recognition
   - Start each day with one affirming statement
   - Leave an uplifting sticky note for your partner to see
2. **Empathic Words** - the Language of Presence
   - Check in daily by asking how your partner feels
   - Mirror their emotions when they share i.e. *'That sounds difficult'*
3. **Clear Words** - the Language of Safety
   - Share one clear need for the next day i.e. *'I'll need your help with...'*
   - Practice stating requests directly, without hints
4. **Repairing Words** - the Language of Healing
   - If you speak harshly, apologise within an hour
   - Ask before bed if there's anything you need to repair
5. **Curious Words** - the Language of Discovery
   - Ask your partner one open-ended question daily
   - Once a week, discuss a bigger question or dream
6. **Visionary Words** - the Language of Hope
   - Express shared gratitude each evening
   - Speak positively about your shared future daily

Figure 11.1 Relationship rhythms

Tools for Busy Seasons

Micro-Habits for Connection

Life doesn't always allow for long, reflective conversations. But it's during busy, stressful and chaotic periods that the relationship is most vulnerable to drifting apart. To ensure your daily rhythm doesn't collapse under pressure, couples must master micro-habits: small, repeatable actions that keep the connection alive with minimal investment in time or energy.

Table 11.2 Micro-habits for connection

Micro-Habit	Language Focus	How It Works
Two-minute rule	Affirming and empathic words	Commit to spending at least two focused minutes daily. This could be a 120-second hug, a brief expression of gratitude or simply listening to a partner's quick offload without interruption. Quality over quantity ensures neither partner feels forgotten
Sticky note affirmations	Affirming words	Leave short, targeted notes (clear words) where your partner will find them – on the bathroom mirror, in a lunch bag or on the steering wheel. Focus on celebrating their character or efforts: 'Loved how you handled the meeting today'
Repair codes	Repairing words	Agree on a simple, non-aggressive phrase (e.g. 'Start again?' or 'Code Yellow') to signal the need for a momentary pause and a tone check. This allows one person to trigger a quick repair without starting a new argument
Question cards	Curious and visionary words	Keep a deck of pre-written, open-ended curiosity questions handy (e.g. 'What's one thing you're looking forward to this week?'). Pull one out while waiting for dinner or driving to an errand, ensuring every spare moment is an opportunity for discovery

By mastering these micro-tools, you ensure your relationship has a safety net of connection, even when you're running on empty.

Practical Exercises

Build Your Rhythm Plan

Write down your plan. Post it somewhere visible. Commit to trying it for 30 days, then review it together.

1. Daily: choose one touchpoint (morning, midday, evening).
2. Weekly: schedule one check-in time.
3. Monthly: plan one date or intentional activity.
4. Annually: set aside one half-day for deeper reflection.

Keep it realistic. Small steps are the most sustainable steps. Revisit after one month to see what's working.

> " Small daily rhythms prevent large relational ruptures

Obstacles to Rhythm: Defeating the Drift

Adopting new, healthy communication habits is rarely a smooth process. Even with the best tools, couples face internal and external resistance that threatens to derail the consistency of their rhythms. Overcoming these obstacles requires far more than willpower; it demands grace and intentionality.

1. Busyness: urgent excuse

- ♥ The most common enemy of rhythm is the feeling of being 'too busy.' When life fills with work, chores and deadlines, dedicated connection time is often the first thing cut. This creates a destructive paradox as the moment a couple feels too busy is precisely the moment such habits as the daily check-in are needed most to manage stress and prevent drift.
    - o Counter-tactic: reframe your rhythm time not as another chore, but as a non-negotiable investment in efficiency. You aren't wasting time; you're saving the countless hours that would otherwise be spent on conflict, resentment and misunderstanding.

2. Perfectionism: all-or-nothing trap

- ♥ The pursuit of a flawlessness is the fastest route to giving up entirely. Perfectionism tells couples that if they once miss their weekly audit, or if a conversation isn't perfectly empathic, the entire rhythm is a failure. This all-or-nothing thinking leads to shame and abandoning the practice.
    - o Counter-tactic: embrace the principle of 'good enough is better than perfect.' The goal is not rigid adherence to a schedule, but intentional presence. If you miss a day, simply resume the rhythm the next. The value is in the consistency of the return, not the absence of a lapse.

3. Disconnection: misaligned expectations

- ♥ Trying to implement a new rhythm (like the monthly momentum check-in) without discussing what each partner truly values within that time creates early disconnection. If one partner views the time as a task-list review (clarity), while the other views it as an opportunity for deep emotional sharing (curiosity), the interaction will have failed before it starts.

- Counter-tactic: use clear and curious words to co-create the rhythm. Before starting, ask: 'What is the primary emotional purpose of this time for you?' Ensure the rhythm explicitly addresses the highest priority need for both partners.

The commitment to rhythm means accepting that there will be mistakes and interruptions.

The victory is not in achieving a rigid schedule, but demonstrating a resilient, shared intentionality to come back to the language of connection, no matter how chaotic life becomes.

Relationship Transformed by Rhythm

When I met Samson and Ally, they described their marriage as 'functional but flat'. They rarely fought but also rarely connected deeply. After they introduced a daily affirmation and a weekly check-in, their connection grew rapidly.

Ally reflected, 'The structure gave us something to lean on. It wasn't about grand gestures; it was about small, steady rhythms that made love visible.'

> Routine words can carry eternal weight

Reflection Questions

- Which of these rhythms feels most natural to us?
- Which ones would stretch us the most?

- ♥ What daily or weekly practice could we start this week without overwhelming ourselves?
- ♥ Which rhythms currently shape our relationship, for better or worse?
- ♥ Do we lean more toward spontaneous moments or consistent practices?
- ♥ Which daily or weekly rhythm would help us most right now?
- ♥ How might these rhythms protect us from drifting apart?

Closing Thought

There is a power in consistency. Love is not sustained by accident; it is built rhythmically, brick by intentional brick.

We now understand that a thriving relationship doesn't depend on rare, intense bursts of emotion, but on the steady, consistent pulse of connection. The six emotionally intelligent languages are not a collection of one-time techniques; they are daily choices that redefine what it means to be present with your partner.

By weaving these practices – from the two-minute rule to the annual vision audit – into the ordinary fabric of life, couples forge a quiet, extraordinary resilience. Yes, big declarations and grand gestures matter in the moment, but it is the daily drops of intentional words and the consistent practices that sustain love in the long run.

Your commitment to these rhythms is the promise that your love will not only endure but flourish, transforming your shared life into a masterpiece of continuous connection.

In essence, the language of consistency has a rhythm that says, 'We choose love again and again – every day.'

12. High-Stakes Conflict

Why High-Stakes Conflict Matters

Every couple knows the gut-wrenching dread of a high-stakes conflict. These are not the gentle arguments over who left the lights on; these are the existential battles that touch the raw nerves of your shared life – money, in-laws, trust or chronic intimacy issues. They feel less like a discussion and more like a seismic event, threatening to crack the very foundation of your partnership.

Retreat to the Primitive Script

In these crucial moments, your brain's alarm system – the amygdala – takes over. Fear floods your body with adrenaline, triggering the primal impulse to fight, flee or freeze. This is why all the thoughtful, intentional languages you've worked so hard to cultivate suddenly vanish. When the stakes are highest, we stop listening, we stop thinking with empathy, and we regress to our most basic, reactive and often destructive scripts. We shift from connection to self-protection and the consequences are devastating: trust erodes, resentment hardens and the wall of dialogue becomes impenetrable.

But I must clarify a fundamental truth: conflict, as painful as it is, is not a failure of love; it is merely a sign of unmet needs fighting to be heard.

Roadmap to Resilience

The true measure of your relationship's resilience is not in avoiding these conflicts, but in how quickly and intentionally you choose to repair the damage once the struggle subsides. This chapter is your field guide to navigating those emotional pressure points, where you affirm, 'I will abandon the corrosive goal of winning the argument and shift the entire focus to understanding the rupture.'

Here is a step-by-step path that forces you out of reaction and into intention, based on the following concepts:

- ♥ De-escalation: mastering time out to halt destructive behaviour before damage is done
- ♥ Immediate repair: using sincere repairing words to mend wounds and restore emotional safety
- ♥ Root resolution: applying curious and clear words to solve the underlying chronic issue, ensuring the argument doesn't recycle.

This chapter moves the six languages from being a set of helpful tools to becoming a life raft, providing the structure and safety needed to stay connected when you both feel most alone. By controlling the conflict, you prove that your love is bigger than your disagreement.

De-escalation Protocol: Calling an Emotional Time Out

When a high-stakes conflict escalates, the rational part of the brain shuts down. Continuing to argue in this state guarantees that damage will be done. Time out is not an escape tactic; it is a mutual commitment to halt destruction and to return to the conversation once you can speak with respect. There are three stages to a time out:

Stage 1. Recognise and Withdraw (Internal Check)

Start with an internal, non-verbal action of recognising your own emotional saturation.

- ♥ Flood: the moment you feel your emotional system is 'flooded' – heart racing, hands shaking, thoughts spiralling toward contempt or withdrawal – you must immediately signal for the pause.
- ♥ Rule of pause: if neither partner can speak using empathic or clear words, they must stop speaking altogether. You can physically turn away or put your hand up as a non-verbal cue, but the next stage must follow instantly.

Stage 2. Declare the Need (Clear Words and Respect)

The critical second step is to announce the pause using non-blaming language. The use of clear words stops the spiral.

- ♥ Use agreed phrase: employ a pre-agreed, low-stress phrase that signals a strategic retreat, not an abandonment
    - o Effective examples – 'I'm feeling flooded and need a time out so I can hear you properly later' or 'My brain is shutting down; let's hit the pause button.'

- o Avoid – 'I'm done with this' or 'You're shouting/ yelling too much', which are accusatory phrases and increase escalation

- ♥ Commit to safety: the listening partner must accept the time out instantly and gracefully, respecting the need for space. Resistance or pursuit during a time out is a serious breach of trust.

Stage 3. Define the Return (Clarity and Repair)

Time out only works if there is a clear commitment to resuming the discussion. If the return is ambiguous, it feels like rejection and prevents repair.

- ♥ Re-scheduling: before physically separating, set a specific time to return to the issue. Be specific, use clear words (e.g. 'I need 30 minutes to calm myself. Can we agree to meet back here at 7.45 p.m.?').
- ♥ Calming ritual: use the time for self-soothing, non-ruminative activities (e.g. listening to music, reading a book, walking, meditating). Avoid rehearsing your defence or blaming your partner in your head, as this defeats the purpose of the time out.

The effectiveness of this protocol is measured by your mutual dedication to the agreed-upon return time, reinforcing that the relationship is safe even amid high-stakes emotional turbulence.

Path Back: Two Tools for Intentional Recovery

Successfully navigating a high-stakes conflict requires moving from damage control to deep resolution. We use two powerful, post-conflict tools to help couples establish a clear, intentional path back to connection after emotional turbulence: post-conflict repair huddle; and conflict dissection.

1. Post-Conflict Repair Huddle: Mending the Wound

This is an essential first step after a time out that focuses exclusively on emotional triage. Its purpose is to prioritise the relationship's safety over the fight's content.

When an argument escalates, the greatest damage often comes not from *what* you were fighting about, but *how* you fought – the harsh words, the defensiveness or the contempt. The repair huddle uses repairing and empathic words to quickly clean up that emotional wreckage.

- ♥ Focus: damage done to the partner, not the issue that caused the fight
- ♥ Goal: to acknowledge and apologise for personal failures in communication (tone, volume, name-calling) and to restore the fundamental belief that the relationship is safe, regardless of disagreement. It quickly re-establishes trust, ensuring that a painful memory doesn't fester into a long-term resentment.

2. Conflict Dissection: Solving the Chronic Problem

Once emotional safety is restored through the repair huddle, you can move to the strategic work of conflict dissection. This tool analyses chronic issues; those arguments you have over and over (money, chores, etc.).

- ♥ Focus: the root cause and the unmet need driving the recurring conflict
- ♥ Goal: to move past the surface fact (e.g. 'The kitchen is messy') by using curious words to uncover the deeper emotional truth (e.g. 'I need to feel my labour is respected'). By shifting the frame from blame to unmet needs, this process transforms a chronic argument into a solvable problem. Clear words build a concrete, mutually acceptable plan, while visionary words ensure that the new solution aligns with the kind of partnership you both want to create.

Together, these tools provide a complete lifecycle for conflict: the huddle heals the *person*, the dissection solves the *problem*. They ensure that every fight, no matter how intense, ultimately leads to a deeper foundation of trust and understanding.

How the Post-Conflict Repair Huddle Works

The single most important factor in relationship resilience is not the absence of fighting, but the speed and sincerity of the repair. This huddle is a short session focused purely on mending the emotional rupture created by the conflict. It uses repairing words to rebuild safety.

1. Own the Damage (Sincere Apology)

Repair must begin with one or both partners acknowledging their personal contribution to the damage, even if they disagree on the root issue. This requires prioritising the relationship over being 'right.'

- ♥ Specific apology: Use repairing words to apologise only for your own destructive actions (e.g. tone, volume, interrupting, name-calling, walking out)
    - o Instead of 'I'm sorry I shouted/yelled, but you made me angry,' which is conditional
    - o Try 'I apologise for my tone and for raising my voice. That was unnecessary and hurt you. I regret that.'
- ♥ Acknowledge the intent: the listening partner should use empathic words to accept the apology without immediately reigniting the conflict. A simple 'thank you, I accept that' is sufficient.

2. Name the Wound (Empathy and Clarity)

Once the initial repair is made, briefly revisit the emotional damage caused by the conflict, not the subject of the conflict itself.

- ♥ Partner A asks for clear words: 'What was the most painful thing I said or did when we were arguing?'
- ♥ Partner B uses clear words to state the damage factually and clearly: 'When you walked out without setting a return time, I felt abandoned and frightened.'
- ♥ Partner A validates by acknowledging their pain with empathic words: 'I understand why you felt abandoned. I see that now, and I am sorry I caused you that fear.' Validation must precede any attempt to explain your behaviour.

3. Future-Proofing (Vision and Action)

Conclude the huddle by committing to a small, tangible action that prevents the same kind of damage in the next conflict. This is where visionary words create a better future.

- New rule: agree on one clear, actionable rule for the next difficult conversation, such as, 'Next time I feel flooded, I will only use the agreed-upon phrase, and I will write down the return time on a note for you.'
- Reaffirm commitment: end the session by physically reconnecting (a hug, holding hands) and verbally reinforcing your commitment to the long-term partnership. 'We got through that. I'm with you and we'll keep practising this.'

This structured approach transforms the aftermath of a fight from a silent, lingering resentment into a purposeful, trust-building moment. The post-conflict repair huddle is a vital tool that gives couples a clear, intentional path back to connection after a high-stakes conflict.

How Conflict Dissection Works to Solve Chronic Issues

If you find yourselves fighting about the same thing every month (money, chores, screen time, etc.), the problem isn't the issue itself; it's the unmet need that keeps driving the argument.

Conflict dissection is a structured exercise designed to move the conversation from 'You did X' to 'We need Y.'

1. Identify the Loop (Clarity)

Start the session (ideally when calm) by using clear words to name the recurring pattern, focusing on the *observable outcome*, not the blame:

- o Instead of 'We always fight because you're messy'
- o Try 'We keep getting stuck in a clean-up loop, where one of us gets resentful about the state of the kitchen. Let's solve this loop.'

2. Name the Unmet Need (Curiosity and Empathy)

This is the most critical step. The goal is to ask curious words that uncover the deeper emotional need driving the frustration.

- ♥ Partner A asks, 'When we are arguing about this, what do you truly need that you aren't currently getting?'
- ♥ Partner B responds by moving beyond the surface fact
    - o Surface fact: 'I need you to take the rubbish out.'
    - o Underlying need, the true problem: 'When I feel solely responsible for the house, I don't feel like your equal partner. I need to feel that our labour is balanced.'
- ♥ Validate: the listening partner must validate the need using empathic words before offering any solution, 'I hear that you need to feel balanced and respected in your labour. That makes perfect sense.'

3. Co-Create the Solution (Vision and Action)

Once the underlying need is clear, you can shift into collaborative problem-solving, using visionary words to plan a better future.

- ♥ Brainstorming (affirmation): generate 3–5 possible solutions together. Encourage even silly ideas. Affirm the partner's input and teamwork, 'I love that idea; let's write it down'

- Commitment to action (clear words): choose one solution you both genuinely agree on and turn it into a concrete, measurable plan, such as, 'We agree that every day at 7.00 p.m., we spend 10 minutes cleaning the kitchen together as a team.'
- Schedule a review: use clear words to commit to checking in on this new solution during your next weekly alignment check-in.

By dissecting the conflict, you stop reacting to the symptoms and start healing the root cause, making it a true opportunity for growth.

Navigating the Financial Minefield

Bosun and Esther had always struggled with money talk. It wasn't about a lack of income, but about different philosophies: Bosun was a saver, Esther a planner who enjoyed experiences. This difference often flared into high-stakes arguments, particularly around unexpected expenses.

Trigger: Broken Washing Machine

One Tuesday, their washing machine died. A perfectly ordinary, but very expensive, household crisis.

'It's going to cost us at least five hundred quid, probably more,' Esther sighed, looking at Bosun. 'I saw a sale on a new, energy-efficient model online – we could have it delivered by Friday.'

Bosun bristled. 'Five hundred quid? Just like that? We just paid for the car service, and you bought those theatre tickets last week! Can't we try fixing it first? We always rush into these things.' His voice, although not yelling, had an edge that implied blame.

Esther felt a familiar wall go up. 'Rush into things? I'm trying to be proactive. You'd rather sit with smelly clothes for a week while you "think about it". Sometimes I feel like you just assume I'm frivolous with our money!' Her voice began to rise.

Seeing Esther's face tighten and feeling his own heart race, Bosun remembered their de-escalation protocol. He raised a hand slightly. 'Okay, wait. I'm feeling flooded. My brain is going into overdrive. I need a time out so we can talk about this better later.'

Esther, though still fuming, nodded curtly. They had agreed to this. 'Fine,' she snapped, 'but can we talk tonight after dinner? Before 9 p.m.?'

'Yes,' Bosun agreed. '7:30 in the living room.'

They separated.

Bosun went for a walk, listening to an audiobook. Esther took a long bath, consciously trying not to rehearse her arguments.

Phase 1: Post-Conflict Repair Huddle

At 7.30 p.m., they met, both calmer but still a little tense.

'Okay,' Bosun started, remembering his script. 'I want to start by apologising for my tone when we were talking earlier. I know my voice had an edge, and it sounded like I was blaming you for trying to find a solution. That was unfair and I regret that.'

Esther softened slightly. 'Thank you, Bosun. I accept that. I also need to apologise. When you sounded like that, I got defensive and snapped. My comment about you "sitting with smelly clothes" was unkind, and I'm sorry for that.'

'I accept your apology too,' Bosun said. He then took the next step in their huddle. 'What was the most painful thing I said or did when we were arguing?'

Esther hesitated, then said, 'When you said, "We always rush into these things" right after I mentioned the theatre tickets. It made me feel like you think I'm irresponsible with our joint money, and it really stung.'

Bosun nodded. 'I understand why you felt that. I can see how those words, especially after you'd just planned something fun, would make you feel criticised and undervalued. I am truly sorry I caused you that feeling.' He didn't defend his *intention*; he validated her *impact*.

'Thank you,' Esther said, genuinely. 'I felt the same when you implied I'm frivolous. It makes me feel like you don't trust my judgement.'

'I hear that,' Bosun replied. 'I need you to know I do trust your judgement, and my words didn't reflect that.' He then concluded with their agreed-upon future-proofing step. 'Next time, I'll try to just state my concern about the cost, instead of layering it with other examples or implying blame. How does that sound?'

'That would help a lot,' Esther agreed. They reached across the sofa and held hands, the immediate emotional damage mended.

Phase 2: Conflict Dissection

The next evening, with the emotional air clear, they revisited the washing machine dilemma, but with a new approach.

'Okay,' Esther began. 'We clearly have a chronic "money surprise" loop. We always argue when an unexpected large expense comes up. What do you truly need that you aren't currently getting when these things happen?'

Bosun thought for a moment. 'When a big expense hits and we haven't discussed it, I immediately feel a loss of control. It's not about the money itself as much as the feeling of being blindsided. I need to feel like we're always seeing the big financial picture together, even for these emergencies.' His deeper need was for clarity and vision.

Esther listened intently. 'I hear that, Bosun. You need to feel like you have a clear, shared picture of our finances and that you're not blindsided by big decisions. That makes perfect sense. I get that.'

Then it was Esther's turn. 'When these things come up, what I'm truly needing is to feel like we're a proactive team. I need to feel that my research and quick-thinking are valued, not criticised. I want to feel like we can make swift, effective decisions together, not just react slowly.' Her deeper need was for affirmation and teamwork.

Bosun validated her. 'I hear you need to feel like your proactiveness is valued and that we're a swift, effective team. I understand that. My behaviour wasn't showing you that.'

Now, with both underlying needs exposed (Bosun's need for shared financial clarity and Esther's need for valued proactiveness), they could co-create solutions.

They brainstormed:

- ♥ 'What if we have a small emergency fund just for household breakdowns?'
- ♥ 'What if we have a quick "expense huddle" for anything over £200, no matter what?'
- ♥ 'What if we each have a discretionary spend amount we don't have to justify?'

They settled on two solutions:

1. Household emergency pot: they'd allocate a small, fixed amount each month to an emergency savings account specifically for things like the washing machine, which addressed Bosun's need for predictability
2. Decision time window: for any expense over £200, they'd agree to a 3-hour decision window. Esther could

research, Bosun could process, and they'd decide together within that time. This addressed Esther's need for efficiency and Bosun's need for consultation.

'So, for the washing machine, Esther can find the best model, and we'll both look at the specs and price together within three hours tonight,' Bosun summarised.

'Perfect,' Esther smiled. 'That feels much better.'

They agreed to review these new rules in their next weekly alignment check-in. The washing machine was still broken, but their ability to navigate such challenges was now significantly stronger, thanks to the integrated power of their six languages.

Reflection Questions

Conflict is one of the most powerful teachers in a relationship. Use these questions to reflect individually or discuss them calmly with your partner after the conflict has been fully resolved and repaired.

- ♥ De-escalation: in our last high-stakes argument, what was the first clear sign that I was becoming flooded? What specific action could I have taken 30 seconds earlier to call a time out?
- ♥ Empathy: what was the deepest, most painful unmet need my partner was communicating during that fight? Was it a need for respect, security, appreciation, or something else?
- ♥ Repairing words: did I apologise only for my tone and behaviour, or did I accidentally sabotage my apology by defending my intentions ('I'm sorry, but ...')? How quickly did we move to sincerely mend the emotional rupture?

- Clarity and vision: if this was a recurring fight, what single, concrete rule or system (like an agreed-upon household fund or responsibility chart) could we create to prevent this exact argument from starting again?
- Self-accountability: if I'm honest, am I more focused on winning the argument or on understanding my partner? What is one specific thing I will commit to practising in our next difficult conversation?

Closing Thought

The courage of a resilient relationship is not proven in calm, but in the heat of conflict. It takes remarkable courage to look at a partner when you are both emotionally wounded and choose repair over retreat, empathy over defence and clarity over contempt.

Remember this fundamental truth: you are not fighting against your partner; you are fighting alongside them against a shared problem.

The ability to successfully navigate conflict – to call time out, mend the wound with a huddle and solve the chronic issue with dissection – transforms it from a destructive force into your most profound proof of commitment. These tools teach you that even when the stakes are highest, the six languages will serve as your bedrock, proving again and again that your love is stronger than your disagreement.

In essence, the language of conflict dissection de-escalates to say, 'We are not fighting against each other, we are fighting for our unmet needs.'

13. Real-Life Stories

Why Stories Matter

Principles and tools are vital, but stories are what stick. They allow us to see ourselves in others, to learn through example and to believe that change is possible. The following seven stories from the frontline illustrate how couples have applied the six emotionally intelligent languages in everyday life (to protect the couples' identities we have used fictitious names). While the details vary, the theme is the same: words can transform relationships.

> "Your story of change can be the inspiration someone else is waiting for

Story 1. Power of Affirming Words

Background

Rachel and Dan had been married for eight years. They loved each other deeply, but somewhere along the way they had slipped into autopilot. Their conversations often revolved around logistics – school runs, bills and chores – and while criticism came easily, compliments had become rare. Dan felt unappreciated, while Rachel longed to feel noticed. Both cared, but neither expressed it.

Breakthrough

After learning about the Daily Three (see Chapter 3), Rachel decided to give it a try. Each night before bed, she affirmed Dan for three things – sometimes big, 'Thank you for working so hard for our family,' sometimes small, 'I loved how you made me laugh tonight.'

At first, Dan brushed it off, unsure how to respond. But over the following weeks, something shifted. The words began to sink in. He not only softened in his responses but also started affirming Rachel in return, often catching her by surprise with his own observations and gratitude.

Result

The change was subtle at first, but it built quickly. Their home began to feel lighter and warmer. Rachel described it this way: 'I feel noticed again, like the little things I do actually matter.' Dan added, 'I didn't realise how much I needed to hear her words too. Her affirming words reminded me of the good between us.'

Commentary

What began as a small nightly practice became a turning point. Affirming words shifted the atmosphere of their relationship from criticism to appreciation, creating a new emotional climate in which love felt spoken, not just assumed.

Story 2. Healing Through Empathy

Background

Sophie and Mark loved each other, but their differences in handling stress often pulled them apart. Mark liked to process things out loud, talking through problems until he found clarity. Sophie, on the other hand, tended to shut down when she felt overwhelmed, needing space before she could open up. This mismatch created tension. Mark felt shut out and unwanted, while Sophie felt pressured and misunderstood. Their arguments often ended in frustration as Sophie retreated into silence, while Mark kept demanding answers she wasn't ready to give.

Breakthrough

After learning about empathic words, Mark decided to change his approach. One evening Sophie came home visibly upset after a difficult day at work. Normally, Mark would have launched into a series of questions: 'What happened? Why are you upset? What can I do?' But this time, he paused. Gently, he said, 'It looks like today was really heavy for you. I just want you to know I'm here.'

Those words landed differently. Sophie didn't feel interrogated or pressured; she felt understood. There was no demand to explain, only the safety of being seen. Over the weeks that followed, Mark continued to practise empathic words by naming Sophie's emotions and sitting with her in them, rather than trying to fix or solve them.

Result

The shift was profound. Sophie later said, 'I finally felt safe to let him in, because he wasn't trying to fix me – he was just being with me.' Mark reflected, 'I realised empathy doesn't mean I have to solve her problems. It means she doesn't have to face them alone.'

Commentary

Their connection deepened, not because life became less stressful, but because Sophie no longer carried her burdens in silence. Empathic words turned what used to be a cycle of frustration into moments of shared presence, reminding both that love is not about quick fixes but about walking together through the weight of life.

Empathy bridges the gap between two different ways of coping. For Sophie and Mark, it transformed pressure into presence and distance into closeness. When couples practise empathic words, they discover that healing often begins not with solutions, but with understanding.

Story 3. Clarity Preventing Crisis

Background

Wale and Buki often found themselves stuck in the same cycle of arguments about household responsibilities. The fights were never explosive, but they were draining. Buki would drop hints about feeling overwhelmed, hoping Wale would notice, while Wale assumed silence meant everything was fine.

When frustration finally bubbled over, it came out as sharp words. Afterwards, both would retreat to separate rooms, waiting for the other to break the silence. This cold distance could go on for days, leaving both resentful and disconnected.

Breakthrough

After yet another tense exchange, Buki remembered what they had been learning about the power of clarity. Instead of retreating, she chose a different approach. Sitting down with Wale, she said plainly but gently: 'I need your help with the household responsibilities. Could you take care of the laundry this week, so I don't feel so stretched?'

Wale was caught off guard – not by her request, but by how straightforward it was. For the first time, he didn't have to guess at what she wanted. He responded, 'Thank you for saying it like that. I can definitely do that.' The tension dissolved almost instantly.

Result

Buki later reflected, 'I realised I'd been expecting him to read my mind. Once I said it clearly, it felt like a weight lifted.' Wale added, 'I wasn't ignoring her. I just didn't know exactly what she wanted. Clear words gave me a chance to show up.'

Commentary

By choosing clear words over hints, Buki prevented what could have turned into another drawn-out silence. Their conversation lasted minutes, not days, and ended with understanding rather than resentment.

The language of safety uses clear words to remove guesswork and assumptions. For Wale and Buki, a simple clear request replaced tension with teamwork. It showed them that honesty spoken with kindness can prevent small issues from becoming crises.

Story 4. Repair to Save Marriage

Background

Aaron and Lisa had been married for over a decade, but the last few years had been marked by distance and resentment. Their arguments weren't just about small things – they often touched raw nerves, leaving wounds that lingered for days. Silence became their default response, with neither willing to apologise. They still lived under the same roof, but their hearts felt miles apart. Separation had quietly entered the conversation.

Breakthrough

Everything began to shift when they came across the Anatomy

of a Good Apology (see Chapter 6) during a counselling session. Aaron realised he had been waiting for Lisa to make the first move, while all along his silence was deepening her hurt. One evening, after yet another strained dinner, he finally broke the cycle. With trembling words, he said: 'I was wrong to shut you out. I see how it hurt you. I want to do better.'

Lisa froze, tears welling in her eyes. For the first time in years, she felt seen, not blamed. She whispered back through sobs: 'I forgive you.'

Result

They later described that evening as the turning point of their marriage. It didn't erase years of pain overnight, but it cracked open a door they thought had closed for good. Over the weeks that followed, they began to practise repairing words more often. Apologies no longer felt like losing ground, but like reclaiming lost intimacy.

Lisa reflected, 'That was the first moment I believed we could find our way back.' Aaron added, 'I thought saying sorry would make me look weak. But it turned out to be the strongest thing I'd ever done.'

Commentary

Repairing words don't erase conflict, they transform it. For Aaron and Lisa, one vulnerable apology became the spark that reignited hope. Their story reminds us that repairing words are not about perfection, but about the courage to take that first step back toward one another.

> Every story proves the same truth: words can wound, but they can also heal

Story 5. Rediscovering Curiosity

Background

Funke and Chris had been together for 15 years. They loved one another deeply, but their conversations had slowly narrowed into a cycle of logistics – bills to be paid, school schedules for the children, and the never-ending to-do list of everyday life. The spark of discovery they once felt in their dating days had been replaced with a sense of routine. Both felt safe in the relationship, but also a little stuck, as though they already knew everything there was to know about each other.

Breakthrough

After several counselling sessions they decided to try something new – a Question Jar (see Chapter 7). They each wrote down a handful of open-ended questions, placed them in a jar and agreed to pull one out each week over coffee or dinner.

One evening, Chris pulled out the question: 'What's something you've always wanted to try but haven't yet?' Funke hesitated at first, then confessed a long-held dream: 'I've always wanted to learn to paint.' Chris was surprised, he had never heard her say that before. Rather than brushing it aside, he encouraged her to pursue it. A few days later, he even brought home a starter set of brushes, canvases and paints.

Result

That simple exchange lit something new in their marriage. Funke later said, 'It felt like he saw a new part of me, and it reminded me that I'm still growing, not just surviving.' Chris added, 'I realised there's still so much to discover about her.

Even after 15 years, she's not a finished book – she's a story still unfolding.'

Commentary

Their curiosity didn't just lead to painting lessons; it refreshed their bond. It reminded them both that discovery doesn't end with commitment. By practicing curious words, they found fresh ways to see and celebrate one another, keeping their love dynamic and alive.

Curiosity is an oxygen for long-term relationships; it prevents stagnation and keeps love breathing. Funke and Chris discovered that even small, playful practices such as a Question Jar can reignite wonder, showing that there is always more to learn, more to explore and more to love in one another.

Story 6. Power of Shared Vision

Background

Imani and Joel had been married for several years and, while their relationship was steady, both quietly felt stuck. Their days had become predictable: wake up, work, eat dinner, watch TV, have sex (twice a month), sleep, repeat. Their conversations revolved mostly around logistics – who would pick up the groceries, how to juggle schedules, what bills needed paying. Nothing was 'wrong,' but both sensed something was missing. They weren't moving backward, but they also weren't moving forward.

Breakthrough

One evening, after a particularly dull week, they decided to try something new: a Vision Night (see Chapter 8). They lit candles, brewed tea and set aside their phones. The goal wasn't to solve problems but to dream about the future.

As they talked, Joel admitted something he'd never voiced before: 'I want us to save for travel. I don't just want to talk about going places, I want us to actually see the world together.'

Imani lit up. She shared her own desire: 'I've been thinking about volunteering together, maybe at a community project or overseas. I want us to do something meaningful side by side.'

They began to sketch out a five-year plan, setting aside small savings for travel and exploring local volunteer opportunities. For the first time in years, they felt like co-authors of a story bigger than their daily routine.

Result

Joel reflected, 'We finally had something bigger to move toward, not just the day-to-day grind.' Imani added, 'Our vision gave us new energy. It made me excited about us again.'

Commentary

Their Vision Night didn't change their routines overnight, but it changed how they experienced them. Each mundane task – from cooking dinner to saving money – now carried meaning because it was tied to a bigger picture. Visionary words had transformed drift into direction, giving their marriage momentum and purpose again.

Visionary words breathe life into relationships by lifting couples out of the present grind and into future possibility. For Imani and Joel, it wasn't the size of the dream that mattered but the act of dreaming together. A shared vision turns routine into momentum, reminding couples that love is not only about where they are, but also about where they are heading.

Story 7. Integration Through the Compass

Background

Val and Denzel had worked hard on their relationship. They had read books, attended a couples' workshop, and even kept notes on the six emotionally intelligent languages. But when tension arose in real life, theory often went out the window. In the heat of an argument, they found themselves defaulting to old habits, with Val withdrawing and Denzel pressing harder. They both admitted, 'We know the languages matter, but in the moment, we freeze. We don't know which one to use.'

Breakthrough

That changed when they began using the Relational Compass (see Chapter 9). Instead of spiralling, they agreed to pause and ask: 'Which direction do we need right now?'

One evening, after a disagreement about parenting, the conversation started to escalate. Val felt defensive and Denzel felt frustrated. Then, remembering the Relational Compass, Val asked, 'Okay, which direction do we need right now?' Denzel took a breath and replied, 'North. We need affirmation.'

He turned to her and said softly, 'I know you're an amazing mum. I get frustrated, but I don't want you to ever doubt how much I value you.'

The shift was almost immediate. Val's shoulders relaxed, her defensiveness softened and the tension in the room eased. Instead of spiralling into blame, they found a way back to connection.

Result

Reflecting later, Val said, 'The Compass gave us a map. It stopped us from going in circles and helped us find a way forward.' Denzel added, 'I used to feel like I was guessing what to do. Now I feel like we have a guide we can lean on when we get stuck.'

Commentary

Integration is where the six languages come alive. For Val and Denzel, the Relational Compass turned abstract ideas into a practical tool they could use in real time. It reminded them that they didn't need to be perfect – they just needed to pause, choose a direction and take a small step toward connection.

Story Themes

Although each couple's story is unique, common threads emerge:

- Small steps matter – change begins with small, daily practices
- Language shifts climate – when words change, the atmosphere changes
- Breakthroughs follow obstacles – most couples feel resistance before they feel transformation
- Hope is renewed – each couple discovered their relationship was not stuck, it could grow again.

> Stories show us that no couple is alone in their struggles

Vision Night Guide

This is a simple ritual for dreaming together.

Vision night is not about making perfect plans – it's about creating space to dream, align and connect. Here's a simple structure for couples to follow:

Step 1: Set the Scene

- ♥ Choose a relaxed evening when you won't be rushed
- ♥ Create a warm atmosphere – light candles, brew tea, play soft music
- ♥ Put phones away and give each other your full attention.

Step 2: Look Back

- ♥ Share one highlight from the past year or season
- ♥ Acknowledge one challenge you overcame together
- ♥ Use affirming words– 'I loved how you ...' or 'I'm grateful we managed to ...'

Step 3: Dream Forward

Take turns answering prompts, such as:

- ♥ What's one adventure you'd love us to experience?
- ♥ What's a skill or project you'd like us to try together?
- ♥ How do you imagine our relationship growing over the next five years?
- ♥ What kind of legacy do we want to build as a couple?

Encourage each other with curious words. Explore without judgement or rushing to logistics.

Step 4: Create a Shared Vision Statement

Write 2–3 sentences that capture your shared hopes. For example:

- ♥ 'We want to create a home where people feel welcome and loved.'
- ♥ 'We will prioritise time together, no matter how busy life gets.'
- ♥ 'We will invest in travel and experiences that expand our world and bring us closer.'

Step 5: Choose One Action Step

Pick one small, practical action for the coming month that reflects your vision. This could be starting a savings jar, scheduling a date night or researching volunteering opportunities.

Step 6: Celebrate

End the night with gratitude. Share one thing you appreciate about your partner and toast to the future you are building together.

> Transformation becomes believable when seen in anothers life

---

Tip: Repeat a vision night annually or seasonally so that it becomes more than an exercise – it becomes a ritual of hope, direction and unity.

Reflection Questions

- Which of these stories feels most like ours?
- What practices from these couples could we try this week?
- Which of these stories do I relate to most – and why?
- What obstacles in my relationship mirror those described?
- Which emotionally intelligent language might create a breakthrough for us?
- How does hearing others' breakthroughs give us hope for our own journey?

Closing Thought

Stories remind us that we are not alone and that transformation is possible. They show that couples like us – ordinary people with ordinary struggles – can find extraordinary connection through intentional words. Their breakthroughs are a mirror and a map that show us what is possible.

In essence, the language of inspiration uses stories that say, 'If it worked for them, it can also work for us.'

14. Create Your Own Story

Why Your Story Matters

Up until now, we've explored frameworks, tools and real-life stories. You've read about couples who overcame challenges through using affirming words, empathic words, clear words, repairing words, curious words and visionary words. But the most important story is not theirs – it's yours.

No two relationships are the same. Your history, your patterns, your strengths, your struggles, your joys and your dreams for the future are all unique. That uniqueness is what makes your love story irreplaceable.

The six emotionally intelligent languages are not a rigid script to follow. They are not about becoming a 'perfect couple' or copying someone else's journey. Instead, they are a toolkit offering a set of lenses, practices and rhythms that you can adapt to your relationship's needs. This chapter is an invitation to take what you've learned and weave it into the living story you are writing with your partner.

Theory into Practice

Knowledge without practice fades quickly. Many readers finish books inspired but unchanged, any good intentions fading within weeks. Couples who experience transformation are those who put principles into practice, however imperfectly.

To avoid the trap of inspiration without action, consider this four-step pathway:

1. Reflect – take an honest look at your relationship patterns. Where do you already practise these languages naturally? Where do you struggle? Reflection is the mirror that shows you where you are.
2. Experiment – try out the languages in daily life. You don't need to overhaul your relationship overnight. Start small – one affirming word at breakfast, one curious word at dinner, one clear word of request instead of a vague hint. Think of it as experimenting rather than performing.
3. Evaluate – notice what works and what needs adjusting. Did affirming words lighten the mood? Did repairing words cut short an argument? Did curious words spark laughter? Pay attention to the shifts, even if they feel subtle at first.
4. Record – write up your journey as you go. Journaling or even quick notes on your phone can help you track growth over time. Recording your reflections anchors the lessons and reminds you of your progress when challenges come.

Why Reflection and Journaling Matter

Life moves quickly. Without pausing to reflect, insights can slip away and growth can go unnoticed. Taking the time to record your story – whether through journaling, couple conversations or even voice notes – ensures that your progress doesn't vanish in the busyness of daily life.

For some couples, journaling becomes a shared ritual:

writing down affirmations for one another; keeping a 'gratitude log'; or regularly revisiting their vision statement. For others, it's a personal practice, with one partner reflecting privately and then bringing their insights into conversations. There's no right or wrong way. You just need to practice slowing down to notice.

Over time, your reflections become more than notes. They become a record of resilience, proof that you didn't just read about the six languages but lived them. They tell the unfolding story of two people who chose not to drift but to grow.

Your relationship is not a carbon copy of anyone else's – and it's not finished yet. The six languages are tools, but you and your partner are the authors. As you practise, reflect and record, you will discover your own rhythms, your own breakthroughs and that your own story is worth telling.

> The words you practise today will shape the relationship you live tomorrow

Reader Reflection Journal Template

Use this space (weekly or monthly) to track your journey with the six emotionally intelligent languages. Take 10–15 minutes to reflect, write and notice growth.

1. Affirming Words – Language of Recognition

This week, how did I affirm my partner? ________________

When did I feel affirmed? ________________

One affirmation I want to try next week is: ________________

2. Empathic Words – Language of Presence

When did I show empathy to my partner this week? ____________

How did they respond? ____________

One area where I could listen more deeply is: ____________

3. Clear Words – Language of Safety

Did I communicate clearly, or did I rely on hints/assumptions? ____________

How did clarity (or the lack of it) affect us? ____________

One clear request I want to practise this week is: ____________

4. Repairing Words – Language of Healing

Was there a moment I needed to apologise? Did I do it? ____________

How did repair change the atmosphere between us? ____________

One way I can repair quicker next time is: ____________

5. Curious Words – Language of Discovery

What new question did I ask my partner this week? ____________

What did I learn about them? ____________

One question I want to ask next week is: ____________

6. Visionary Words – Language of Hope

Did we talk about our future this week? What inspired us? ____________

How did vision give us energy or direction? ____________

One small step toward our vision is: ____________

Weekly Summary

What felt strongest in our communication this week? ____________

What felt weakest? ____________

One intention I want to carry forward is: ____________

Tip: You don't need to write long essays. Just a few sentences each week can build a powerful record of growth. Over time, you'll see how your words have shaped the climate of your relationship.

> Writing your story is the first step in rewriting your future

Writing Their Own Chapter

Clara and Tom first discovered the six emotionally intelligent languages during one of the hardest seasons of their marriage. Work stress, parenting challenges and constant fatigue left them feeling more like flatmates than partners. Conversations were short, sharp and mostly about logistics. Both admitted later that they were worried they were slowly losing the warmth they once shared.

Instead of giving up, they tried something simple but intentional: they started a shared journal. Every Sunday evening, they would sit together for 20 minutes and write side by side. Some weeks they jotted down affirming words for each other: 'I loved how you encouraged me before my big meeting'. Other weeks, they recorded empathic moments: 'I noticed how tired you were and wanted to thank you for still making time for the kids'. Sometimes they used the journal for apologies, other times for curious questions, and often for dreaming aloud about the future.

At first, the practice felt awkward, almost forced. But over time, the pages filled with words they might never have spoken out loud in the busyness of the week. Looking back through the journal became a reminder of progress – not just the big milestones, but the small steps of kindness, repair and growth that often went unnoticed in the moment.

Clara later reflected, 'It was like writing our love story in real time. Even when we had a bad week, we could look back and see that we were still moving forward, still choosing each other.' Tom added, 'The journal reminded us that love isn't just felt, it's written, remembered and lived.'

A shared journal may seem small, but it turns the invisible work of growth into something tangible. For Clara and Tom, it became more than a notebook – it became a living record of resilience, a reminder that their love story was still unfolding, one page at a time.

Building a Positive Bank Account

Why Joy is a Strategy

Joy, fun and laughter are not luxuries to be scheduled *if* you have spare time; they are proactive, essential tools for a resilient relationship. Many couples make the mistake of focusing solely on fixing what's broken, forgetting that the health of the partnership is measured by its positive experiences.

The renowned relationship research by Dr. John Gottman shows that stable, happy partnerships need a minimum of a 5:1 ratio of positive:negative interactions. Every argument, every stressor and every harsh word cost. Joy and appreciation are the coins you deposit to keep the account healthy.

Affirming Words as Fuel

Think of your connection like a car's engine. Trying to fix a disagreement on an empty tank of goodwill only leads to friction and seizing up. The regular practice of affirming words acts as an emotional fuel, building a deep reservoir of security. By consistently seeing and celebrating your partner's character and effort, you create a buffer against the inevitable shocks of life. This ensures that when conflict does hit, you both trust the intent is good, because the Positive Bank Account is full.

Culture of Appreciation (Affirming Words)

Gratitude should be a consistent pulse, not an occasional splurge. Your intentional use of affirming and clear words creates an atmosphere of respect and warmth in your relationship.

- ♥ Gratitude as a daily habit: move beyond a general 'thanks' to using specific, clear words that highlight your partner's character, which is where the magic lies
    - Instead of 'Thanks for making dinner'
    - Try 'Thank you for the dinner, love. I really appreciate your thoughtfulness in remembering to use the leftovers – it helps us save money and I admire your efficiency' (which affirms their reliability and planning skills, not just the food)
- ♥ Turning toward bids: every time your partner shares a thought, a concern or a joke, they are making a 'bid for connection.' The biggest deposit you can make is to respond with affirming words and attention. If they excitedly show you a funny video or mention a frustrating email, stop what you are doing (even if

only for ten seconds) and turn toward them. That brief moment says: 'You matter more than my distraction.'

> **//** Every couple has a language worth refining

Intimacy Continuum (Curious and Empathic Words)

Intimacy is not a separate event, it is the natural consequence of emotional safety. The path from great conversation to deep physical closeness is a continuum driven by curiosity and empathy.

- ♥ Curiosity is the engine: after years together, it is lethal to assume you know everything about your partner. Curiosity is the engine that fights relationship boredom. It forces you to keep 'dating' the evolving person standing next to you
    - o Schedule deep curiosity checks: ask probing, forward-looking questions to uncover their evolving beliefs and desires, gor example: 'If you could change one non-negotiable family ritual we have, what would it be, and why?'
- ♥ From conversation to closeness: emotional safety is the ultimate aphrodisiac. Physical intimacy thrives when both partners feel safe enough to be vulnerable. Use empathic words to validate desires, concerns and boundaries without judgement. When discussing needs, use non-judgemental clear words. This removes shame and ensures that the conversation about intimacy is built on mutual understanding and respect, not just logistics or duty.

Co-Creating the Fun (Visionary Play)

If your relationship plan only includes managing bills, cleaning the house and raising children, you will become excellent partners in a passionless enterprise. Co-creating the fun is about deliberately using visionary words to plan joy.

- ♥ Shared vision for play: commit to scheduling fun with the same seriousness and budget you apply to your financial goals. Use visionary words to define what 'fun' looks like for your partnership over the next six months. Is it learning to speak Spanish together or a weekend trip to a new city?
    - o Adventure day tool: block out a full Saturday every quarter for a shared activity (hiking, gallery visit, new restaurant) to take you out of your routine
- ♥ Inside jokes and shared meaning: the greatest defence against outside stress is your unique, shared culture. This is the language of inside jokes, private rituals and shared humour, built through years of affirming and clear words. By consistently reinforcing your unique 'us against the world' identity, you forge a stronger, more resilient and infinitely more joyful bond.

> " Your journey is unique, but you don't walk it alone

Continuous Act of Love

You have now completed the deepest work of this journey. You have dismantled the defensive armour of the invisible script, understood its victim counterpart, and learned to wield the six emotionally intelligent languages as tools for connection, not conflict.

However, the final lesson is perhaps the most important: relationship work is not a destination, it is a discipline. This book doesn't offer a cure that makes your relationship impervious to trouble; instead, it provides the resilience required to survive trouble and become stronger afterwards. Love is not a noun to be possessed, it is a verb to be practised.

Finish-Line Myth

Many couples fail because they assume that once they resolve a big issue or achieve a moment of profound connection, the work is over. They fall victim to the 'finish-line myth.'

Relational safety and intimacy, much like physical fitness, require maintenance. If you stop practising affirming words, appreciation fades. If you stop using curious words, your partner slowly becomes a stranger. The continuous act of love is the deliberate choice, every day, to pick up the tools of the six languages and apply them to routine moments, not just to crises.

Shared Ecosystem

Think of the six languages not as isolated skills, but as an interdependent ecosystem that contributes to your relationship's health:

- Affirming words create a positive emotional bank account
- Empathic words ensure the safety to communicate
- Repairing words provide the necessary foundation for resilience

- ♥ Clear words provide the fuel (information) needed for action
- ♥ Curious words prevent stagnation and ensure growth
- ♥ Visionary words guarantee you're still growing in the same direction.

When one language is neglected, the entire system suffers. If you focus on clear words but neglect empathic words, your communication becomes cold and transactional. If you focus on affirming words but neglect repairing words, you are building on a shaky foundation of unresolved resentment.

Transformation to Legacy

Your commitment to learning these languages fundamentally changes how you speak, listen and love.

You have learned to: *speak* with intentionality and accountability (clear and affirming words); *listen* with vulnerability and validation (empathic and curious words); truly *love* with resilience and shared purpose (repairing and visionary words).

The final transformation is the shift from reacting defensively to responding mindfully. It is in this mindful, continuous practice that you move beyond managing your relationship to actively co-creating a legacy of profound emotional intelligence. The work is yours to continue, one word at a time, for the rest of your lives together.

Don't wait for dramatic moments. Your story will be shaped by consistent, ordinary choices. A kind word here, a question there, an apology offered, a dream shared – these create the narrative of your love.

> " Reflection turns insight into transformation

Reflection Questions

- What drew me to this book and what am I hoping to change or strengthen in my relationship?
- Which of the six languages do I find most natural? Least natural?
- How would I describe the current 'emotional climate' of our relationship?
- If we used the Relational Compass this week, which direction would we need most often?
- Looking ahead, what kind of story do I want us to tell in 10 years?

> " Love is not a noun to be possessed;
> it is a verb to be practised

Closing Thought

This book is not the end of your journey. It is the beginning. It can only carry you so far. The six languages are invitations, not instructions. The next chapter belongs to you. The words you choose, the languages you practise, the vision you shape together – these will determine the story you live.

In essence, your relationship is a living story. And the words you speak build the sentences in that story.

15. Conclusion: Love That Lasts

Looking Back, Moving Forward

We've travelled a long journey together:

- ♥ from the foundations of why words matter (Chapter 1)
- ♥ through discovering the six emotionally intelligent languages (Chapters 2–8)
- ♥ to integration (Chapter 9), obstacles and breakthroughs (Chapter 10), rhythms (Chapter 11), high-stakes conflict (Chapter 12) and real-life stories (Chapter 13)
- ♥ and finally, your own journey (Chapter 14).

The thread running through it all is this: love lasts when it is nurtured through intentional words.

Words create climate. Words heal wounds. Words spark curiosity. Words paint vision. And when woven together, words create a relationship that is resilient, intimate and full of hope.

In films and novels, love often looks effortless. Two people meet, sparks fly and 'happily ever after' seems inevitable. But in real life, lasting love is not a straight line. It is a series of daily and deliberate choices. Couples who expect love to be effortless often grow discouraged when challenges arise. But those who understand that love requires intention and practice discover a deeper, richer bond – one that lasts through seasons of both sunshine and storm.

Emotionally intelligent languages provide the tools to make those daily choices.

Myth of Effortless Love

Culture often sells us the idea that love should be easy; that if we're truly meant for each other, everything will fall into place. But lasting love is never effortless. It is not about avoiding storms but learning to navigate them together.

Couples who endure are not those who never argue, but those who repair quickly. They are not those who always know what to say, but those who choose empathy when it matters most. They are not those who coast, but those who remain curious and visionary, even decades in.

Relationship Is Not a Destination, It's a Lifelong Ascent

If you have mastered daily rhythms, navigated high-stakes conflicts and filled your emotional bank account with joy, you have achieved fluency in the six emotionally intelligent languages. But here lies the final, most deceptive trap: the myth of 'The End.'

The truth is, a thriving relationship is not a static state; it is a continuous, lifelong ascent. The moment you believe the work is finished, the process of slow, quiet drift begins. You may be in perfect alignment today, but life's inevitable pressures – career shifts, the departure of children, financial change and the simple fact that you and your partner are constantly changing people – will create new distances tomorrow.

To succeed in the long run, we must shift our visionary

words from surviving the present to proactively scaling the future.

This chapter is your advanced guide to maintaining deep, intentional connection over decades. We will move beyond simply fixing what's broken to actively co-creating a shared future that embraces change. We will use curious words to anticipate the emotional impact of life's transitions, leverage clear words to build flexible blueprints for growth, and ensure our affirming words always celebrate the evolving individual standing beside us. The goal is to make your relationship change-proof – a dynamic, living masterpiece that gets stronger, deeper and more compelling with every passing year.

> " Love that lasts is crafted daily, word by word

Anticipating Major Transitions

Life is inevitably full of challenging moments – the arrival of a child, a major career shift, relocating, the empty nest, coping with illness. Theye are not small bumps in the road; they are major geological shifts that demand couples adapt their roles, routines and identities. When transitions are managed poorly, they amplify existing tensions and become relationship fault lines.

The advanced relational skill is not enduring the transition but anticipating its emotional and logistical impact well in advance. The goal here is to use curious words, clear words and empathic words to build a blueprint for coping with the stressor before it hits.

1. Proactive Curiosity: Mapping Emotional Shifts

The greatest danger during a transition is believing you know how your partner will feel or react. Transitions fundamentally alter a person's identity and priorities. Proactive curiosity means actively updating your internal 'love map' to reflect these changes. So, before the transition (e.g. three months before a move, a year before retirement), schedule a dedicated transition huddle to ask:

- Emotional landscape: 'What are you most excited about, and what is your single biggest fear about this change?' (this validates both joy and anxiety)
- Identity shift: 'What role or routine are you worried about losing in this transition, and what new sense of purpose do you hope to find?' (for a retiree, this helps acknowledge the loss of a professional identity)
- Unknown variables: 'What is one way you predict I will unintentionally fail to support you during this transition?' (when delivered with curious words this question gives permission for pre-emptive vulnerability and allows your partner to express a need you hadn't considered).

> " Affirmation, empathy, clarity, repair, curiosity and vision – these are not techniques, but the grammar of enduring love

2. Clarity Blueprint: Defining New Roles

Major transitions destroy old routines and create a vacuum of responsibility, which often leads to conflict. Clear words fill this vacuum with structure, defining roles and expectations before resentment can set in.

- ♥ Responsibility audit: if the transition involves a major shift in workload (e.g. having a baby or one partner starting a demanding course), use clear words to physically map out the new division of labour. Don't assume. Define who is responsible for logistics, emotional labour and physical tasks
- ♥ Emotional resource budget: acknowledge that emotional energy is finite. If your partner is dealing with high stress demands (e.g. job hunting or caring for an aged parent), use clear words to define the new, temporary 'budget' for time and patience. For example: 'For the next three months, my emotional budget for household stress is only 50 per cent. I need you to lead the planning for our social calendar, and I will focus my energy on [specific task]'
- ♥ Shared metric of success: define what success looks like during the transition. Is it maintaining intimacy? Surviving financially? Use clear words to define a short-term goal to keep the team unified.

3. Empathy During Stress: Validating the Uncomfortable

During a transition, one or both partners are likely to experience exhaustion, moodiness or a loss of identity. This is where empathic words become your most crucial tool for maintaining a safe connection.

- ♥ Validate ambivalence: not all transitions feel good. For instance, parenthood brings not only joy but also intense sleep deprivation and a drop in life satisfaction for many couples. Use empathic words to validate the uncomfortable reality without trying to 'fix' it: 'I know we wanted this move, but it sounds like you're carrying a lot of loneliness right now. It makes sense that you feel overwhelmed, and I'm here to hold that with you.'

- Support individual identity: a transition might push your partner toward a period of self-focus (e.g. needing more time alone to process a job loss). Use empathic words to see the necessity of this individual space, even if it temporarily reduces shared time. Your support of their need to process individually is a profound act of loyalty to their whole self.

By proactively combining curious words to understand feelings, clear words to define plans and empathic words to hold resulting stresses, you transform major life transitions from relationship threats into opportunities for proven, shared resilience.

Fighting Stagnation (Culture of Renewal)

The greatest threat to long-term relationships is often not conflict, but stagnation. When a couple stops actively learning about each other, they risk falling into a comfortable, but ultimately dull, predictability. You stop dating your partner and start co-managing an enterprise. Fighting stagnation requires building a culture of renewal that emphasises continuous curiosity and individual growth.

> " Lasting love is less about sparks and more about steady words

1. Deep Curiosity Check: Dating the Evolving Self

After years together, it's easy to believe you know everything about your partner. This assumption kills intimacy. The reality is that your partner today is not the same person they were a year, or even six months, ago. Deep curiosity is the engine that keeps the connection fresh.

- ♥ Advanced inquiry: move beyond superficial questions about logistics and schedule time to ask high-value, probing questions, designed to uncover evolving beliefs and desires.
  - o Examples: 'What core belief about the world have you changed your mind on recently, and why?' or 'If you could start one new, impractical hobby tomorrow, what would it be, and what does that reveal about your current needs?'
- ♥ New thing metric: commit to learning one genuinely new piece of non-logistical information about your partner every month. This forces you to engage, listen actively with empathy and acknowledge their continuous transformation.

2. Affirming Individual Growth: Preventing Resentment

Relational stagnation often stems from individual stagnation. If one partner feels held back or unseen in their personal pursuits, it breeds resentment that infects the relationship. The strongest partnerships are composed of two whole, thriving individuals.

- Celebrate separate success: use affirming words to sincerely celebrate your partner's successes and efforts outside the relationship (career, friendships, personal challenges). Your role is to be your partner's most dedicated champion
- Support space: use clear words to define and protect the time each partner needs for individual growth, whether it's an evening class, dedicated reading time or a solo weekend trip. Seeing your partner thrive independently makes them a more interesting and energised partner when you reconnect.

3. Novelty Principle: Co-Creating Excitement

The human brain is wired to seek novelty and, when a relationship stops providing it, the mind seeks it elsewhere. Use visionary words to plan activities that challenge your shared routines.

- Plan disruptions: prioritise activities that introduce novelty into your shared experience. This could be learning a new skill together (e.g. pottery or cooking), taking a spontaneous weekend trip to an unfamiliar town, or simply changing the venue for your regular date night
- Shared meaning and humour: a key defence against stagnation is a robust, unique culture of humour, inside jokes and personal rituals, built through years of use of affirming and clear words. These shared meanings serve as a unique, private language that constantly reinforces your sense of 'us' against the stress of the outside world.

By intentionally seeking discovery and supporting each other's evolution, you ensure that the partnership remains a source of enduring excitement, curiosity and vitality, making you a resilient team for the long haul.

The Six Languages as Anchors

Think of the six languages as anchors for the many-sided transitions of life:

- ♥ Affirming words anchor your partner's worth
- ♥ Empathic words anchor their feelings
- ♥ Clear words anchor understanding
- ♥ Repairing words anchor healing
- ♥ Curious words anchor discovery
- ♥ Visionary words anchor hope.

When practised consistently, these anchors hold a relationship steady through stress, change or uncertainty. They are not abstract concepts. In storms, they keep you steady. In calm seas, they keep you connected. Practised together, they become the relational grammar of love that endures.

> " Sustainable love is built in everyday conversations

Love That Endured

I once worked with a couple, Grace and Jonathan, who had been together for over 40 years. When asked their secret, Grace smiled and said, 'We never stopped saying thank you. We never stopped listening. And we never stopped dreaming together.'

Jonathan added, 'We didn't always get it right. But we always came back to each other.'

Their words echo the heart of this book. Love that lasts is not about never failing, it ia about never giving up on practising the languages that bring you back together.

Renewing the Vision

Your relationship's visionary words are not etched in stone; they are drawn in pencil. Over the course of a lifetime, goals and dreams will inevitably shift, priorities will rearrange and the individuals you are will change. The final, essential practice of your progressive partnership is the intentional, periodic renewal of your shared vision. Without this audit, you risk working incredibly hard every day, only to realise years later that you have been pulling toward separate goals.

1. Vision Statement Audit

You must dedicate time to revisiting and updating your collective goal. This audit moves your vision from an abstract idea to a clear, actionable plan for the next phase of your life

- ♥ Schedule a deep dive: use your annual vision audit time or schedule a special visionary weekend every 3–5 years. The goal is to escape the daily chaos and ask the big, challenging questions
- ♥ Foundational question: revisit the core tenets of your partnership. Ask: 'If we looked back five years from now, what three things about our shared life would make us most proud?' This helps you define your new visionary words for your next chapter
- ♥ Alignment test: use clear words to check your alignment with life's major categories. Rate your current satisfaction (1–10) and define a target goal for the next

cycle in areas such as financial strategy, family structure (support for adult children/parents) and lifestyle/travel. Any significant gaps, become your new shared goals.

2. The Legacy of Purpose

In the advanced stages of a long-term partnership, many couples find their greatest fulfilment in a purpose that extends beyond their own lives

- ♥ Defining 'why': use curious words to explore your collective purpose for the decade ahead. This is often framed as legacy. Ask: 'What positive impact do we want our life together to have on our family, community or world?' This gives your day-to-day actions greater meaning.
- ♥ Visionary time allocation: based on your renewed purpose, use clear words to define how to allocate your precious resources of time, money and emotional energy. If your new shared vision includes philanthropic work, define the monthly hours or financial contribution. This ensures your actions constantly reflect your visionary words.

3. Ultimate Affirmation

The final gift the six languages offer is the ability to look at your partner after decades of change, conflict and chaos to affirm the whole journey.

- ♥ Affirmation of resilience: end your vision renewal with a powerful affirmation that celebrates your shared resilience. This is the moment to look back and say, 'Look at what we've built, and look at what we survived.'

- Unending commitment: recommit to the process of growth. The greatest legacy you build together is your vibrant, emotionally intelligent partnership – a living example of resilience to inspire and teach future generations. Your commitment to the lifelong practice of these languages is the ultimate act of love.

Call to Daily Practice

As you close this book, the most important question is not, 'What did I learn?' but 'What will I practise?'

- Will you choose affirming words today, noticing and celebrating the good?
- Will you choose empathic words, listening with presence rather than judgement?
- Will you choose clear words, speaking directly with kindness?
- Will you choose repairing words, humbling yourself to apologise or forgive?
- Will you choose curious words, asking questions that keep your partner known?
- Will you choose visionary words, dreaming and building a future together?

Sustaining Practice

The challenge is not in understanding these languages but in sustaining them. Here are habits to help:

- Keep it small – don't wait for big moments, use micro-moments daily

- ♥ Use the compass – when lost, pause and ask: 'which direction do we need right now?'
- ♥ Review regularly – revisit your six-language plan every few months
- ♥ Seek support – invite mentors, counsellors or trusted friends when help is needed
- ♥ Celebrate progress – acknowledge growth, even if imperfect.

Love is a daily choice. And these six languages are the words that make that choice visible.

Think of love as a language that requires ongoing learning. Just as fluency in any language demands practice, patience and humility, so do emotionally intelligent languages in relationships. There will be seasons of fluency and seasons of struggle. But each word, spoken with intention, adds to the vocabulary of love that sustains you.

Practical Exercise: Your Commitment Statement

Take a blank page and write a short statement beginning with: 'I commit to...'

- ♥ Example: 'I commit to affirming my partner daily.'
- ♥ Example: 'I commit to listening with empathy before offering solutions.'
- ♥ Example: 'I commit to building a shared vision for our future.'

Place it somewhere visible – on your desk, fridge or bedside. Let it remind you daily of the love you are building.

> When words are chosen with care, love becomes a legacy

Reflection Questions

- Which language will I commit to practising more intentionally this week?
- How will I remind myself daily to use the Relational Compass or Emotional Climate Code?
- What do I want our relationship story to sound like in five years?
- What first small step can I take today toward love that lasts?

Closing Vision

This book is not the end of your journey; it is the beginning of a new way of living, speaking and embodying love. The six emotionally intelligent languages are not rigid rules to master but living practices to grow into. They will change with you, stretch with you and deepen as your relationship matures.

You started this journey looking for answers to the frustrating cycle of miscommunication, the unspoken silence of disconnection or the ever-present scare of broken trust. You may have felt trapped behind the wall of dialogue or overwhelmed by the silent emptiness of a quiet drift. Now, you possess not just knowledge, but a complete, working vocabulary for emotional safety: the six emotionally intelligent languages.

You have learned that love is built, not found. It thrives not in rare declarations, but in the daily rhythms you establish. It proves itself not by avoiding conflict, but by the speed and sincerity of the repair afterwards. It is sustained by the proactive joy you build into your shared life and the courage you show in scaling your partnership to face the long ascent of a lifetime.

The languages are simple: affirming words to build worth; empathic words to validate feelings; clear words to set boundaries; curious words to fight stagnation; repairing words to mend wounds; and visionary words to co-create your future.

The heart of this journey has never been about perfection, but about presence. Not about flawless words, but about faithful ones. Not about grand declarations, but about small daily choices that steadily shape the climate of your love.

- ♥ When you choose to affirm, you say: 'I see you'
- ♥ When you choose empathy, you say: 'I am with you'
- ♥ When you choose clarity, you say: 'I want to understand you'
- ♥ When you choose repair, you say: 'I will not let this divide us'
- ♥ When you choose curiosity, you say: 'I still want to know you'
- ♥ When you choose vision, you say: 'I will dream with you and walk beside you into the future.'

These are not just words; they are promises that become habits, and habits that become the story of your life together. Your final challenge is to remember that fluency does not happen by accident; it comes from lifelong practice. You will still misspeak. You will still get angry. You will still feel tired and fall back on old habits.

When this happens – and it will – remember the ultimate act of commitment: the return.

The true measure of your love is not the absence of lapse, but the unwavering resilience of your return to the language of connection. Pick up the rhythm. Use the Repair Huddle. Speak the word that shows your partner they are seen, understood and valued.

Close this book and trust the tools you have absorbed. The greatest legacy you can build together is a resilient, emotionally intelligent partnership, a masterpiece of continuous connection.

Your journey toward lifelong love starts now.

May this book not only inspire you but also accompany you as you write your own love story – one choice, one word, one day at a time.

In essence, love that lasts is love that speaks wisely, kindly and consistently.

> " Let your words become the compass that always leads you back to one another – Sam O. Opeche

Note to Readers

Dear Reader,

Thank you for choosing to spend time with this book. It has been an honour to walk with you through these pages. My hope is that the ideas you've discovered here will not remain as words on paper but will become living practices in your daily life and relationship.

The six emotionally intelligent languages are simple, but they are not always easy. They require courage, vulnerability and consistency. Yet each time you choose them – even imperfectly – you are choosing connection over distance, hope over despair, growth over stagnation. That choice matters more than you may realise.

Please remember that you do not need to master all six languages at once. Start where you are. Practise one small step today. Over time, these steps will weave together into rhythms of love that last.

Your story is still being written. My prayer is that as you practise these languages, you will discover not only greater intimacy with your partner but also greater peace within yourself. May your words be seeds of healing, discovery and vision – a language of love that endures.

Let your words become the compass that always leads you back to one another.

With gratitude and encouragement,

Sam O. Opeche

Appendix of Tools and Resources

A1. Quick-Reference Guide to the Six Languages

Language	Core Message	Sample Phrases	Best Used
Affirming words	'I see you. I value you.'	'Thank you for...' / 'I admire how...'	To strengthen connection and boost morale
Empathic words	'I feel with you.'	'That sounds difficult.' / 'I'm here with you.'	When your partner is upset, stressed or hurting
Clear words	'This is what I mean.'	'I feel... I need...'	To avoid confusion or misinterpretation
Repairing words	'Let's heal and reconnect.'	'I was wrong. I'm sorry.'	After conflict, tension or hurt
Curious words	'I want to know you more.'	'What's on your mind?'	To keep discovery alive and prevent stagnation
Visionary words	'Our future matters.'	'What do we want to build together?'	To set direction, create energy and sustain hope

A2. Emotional Climate Code

A quick tool to gauge the atmosphere of your relationship.

- Sunny – warmth, joy, appreciation
- Cloudy – distance, confusion, lack of clarity

- Stormy – conflict, tension, harsh words
- Calm – safety, presence, understanding
- Fresh – discovery, laughter, new experiences
- Horizon – shared goals, dreaming forward

Daily practice: each evening, ask: 'What was today's emotional climate, and how did my words shape it?'

A3. Relational Compass

A visual, practical way to reorient conversations.

- North – affirmation
- South – repair
- East – curiosity
- West – vision
- Centre – empathy + clarity.

Quick use: in moments of tension, pause and ask, 'Which point of the Compass do we need right now?'

A4. Journaling Prompts

Use these prompts weekly (alone or together):

- What was a highlight in our relationship this week?
- Which of the six languages did I practise well?
- Where did I miss an opportunity?
- What am I most grateful for in my partner right now?
- What is one dream I want us to share?

A5. Sample Weekly Check-In

A 30-minute conversation guide.

5. Affirmation – 'I appreciated when you ...'
6. Empathy – 'This week felt hard because ...'
7. Clarity – 'Something we need to address is ...'
8. Repair – 'I want to apologise for ...'
9. Curiosity – 'A question I'd like to ask is ...'
10. Vision – 'Looking ahead, I'd love us to ...'

A6. Recommended Reading

Chapman, Gary – *The 5 Love Languages*
Gottman, John & Julie – *The Seven Principles for Making Marriage Work*
Brown, Brené – *Dare to Lead* (on clarity and courage)
Siegel, Daniel – *The Whole-Brain Child* (insights on empathy and emotional regulation)
Perel, Esther – *Mating in Captivity* (on curiosity and sustaining intimacy)

A7. Resources for Ongoing Growth

The Reflection Journal – a companion to this book, designed with prompts, exercises, and space to record your personal journey and to track daily and weekly practices with the six emotionally intelligent languages.

Workshops and coaching – live sessions and group workshops that provide couples with hands-on practice and guidance in applying the six languages to their unique circumstances.

Printable tools – downloadable versions of the Relational Compass and Emotional Climate Code for personal or group use.

Speaking engagements – teaching and interactive seminars for churches, conferences or relationship events, based on the principles outlined in this book.

For updates, bookings and resources visit:
www.instagram.com/samopeche
or email
answers.themarriageworkshop@gmail.com

Closing Word

The tools in this Appendix are not meant to add pressure but to provide scaffolding. Use them lightly and flexibly. Adapt them to your unique rhythm as a couple.

Remember: consistency beats intensity. Small daily steps create lasting change.

Bibliography

Underpinning Concepts

Concept in Text	Associated Research Focus	Source
Why joy is a strategy (5:1 ratio)	The 'magic ratio' of five positive interactions for every one negative interaction necessary for relationship stability	Gottman, J. M., & Levenson, R. W. (1992); Gottman, J. M. (1994)
Culture of appreciation (affirming words/bids)	The fundamental unit of emotional communication, focusing on responding positively to a partner's request for attention or affection (Turning Toward)	Gottman, J. M. (1994)
The intimacy continuum (curiosity and empathy)	The necessity of emotional validation and maintaining love maps (a mental map of your partner's inner world) for emotional and physical closeness	Gottman, J. M., & Silver, N. (2012), research by the Gottman Institute on Love Maps
Co-creating the fun (visionary play)	The importance of building rituals of connection and creating shared meaning (goals, values and vision) to navigate life's transitions as a team	Gottman, J. M., & Silver, N. (2012)

Primary Sources

Gottman, J. M. (1994). *Why Marriages Succeed or Fail: And How You Can Make Yours Last*. New York: Simon & Schuster. (Detailed discussion of bids for connection and the emotional bank account concept).

Gottman, J. M., & Levenson, R. W. (1992). 'Marital Processes Predictive of Later Dissolution: Behavior, Physiology, and

Health', *Journal of Personality and Social Psychology*, 63(2), 221–233. (The seminal study that established the predictability of divorce based on interaction patterns).

Gottman, J. M., & Silver, N. (2012). *The Seven Principles for Making Marriage Work: A Practical Guide from the Country's Foremost Relationship Expert*. New York: Harmony Books. (Original research on the 5:1 ratio, the four horsemen and building friendship).

Other Sources

Chapman, Gary. T*he 5 Love Languages: The Secret to Love That Lasts*. Revised edition. Chicago, IL: Northfield Publishing, 2015.

Covey, S. R. (1989). T*he 7 Habits of Highly Effective People: Powerful Lessons in Personal Change*. New York: Simon & Schuster. (Context for the Emotional Bank Account as a metaphor for building trust through small, consistent deposits).

Lyons, Rebekah (2025, May 19). *Building a Marriage That Lasts: Practical Rhythms for Lifelong Connection* [Video] http://www.youtube.com/watch?v=7tLY_CDXdlM

Verywell Mind – www.verywellmind.com

Acknowledgements

This book is the fruit of many conversations, shared stories and lived experiences. My heartfelt thanks go to:

The countless couples who have trusted me to journey with them in therapy and mentoring. Your openness and resilience have inspired much of what is written here.

My colleagues and mentors in the fields of psychotherapy, counselling and restorative practice, whose wisdom and encouragement have shaped my approach.

My family and loved ones, for their constant support, patience and belief in this vision.

And finally, to every reader who dares to invest in their relationship by choosing to practise love with intentionality – this book is for you.

About the Author

Sam Okechukwu Opeche is a qualified psychotherapist and relationship counsellor with a specialised passion for transforming communication breakdowns into lasting connection. With over 15 years of professional experience, Sam has guided countless individuals and couples through the complex challenges of intimacy, conflict and long-term connection.

What sets Sam's work apart is his unique expertise in foundational repair and reconciliation. He has served as a Restorative Justice Facilitator for Essex Police and as a Youth & Family Mentor for Castle Point Council in England, United Kingdom. This unique civic background has given him unparalleled insight into the real-world dynamics of rebuilding trust and finding common ground when the stakes are highest.

Sam's core philosophy is simple: words are not just tools of communication; they are instruments of healing, growth and vision. His writing distils his professional and civic wisdom into a practical framework, making the transformative power of emotionally intelligent language accessible to every couple ready to cultivate a relationship marked by resilience and hope.